CAREFREE

RETREATS

for

ALL

SEASONS

Getaways

PHOTOGRAPHS BY
Jennifer Lévy
AND
Nancy Hill

EDITORIAL ASSISTANCE BY
Carolyn Schultz

CLARKSON POTTER/PUBLISHERS
NEW YORK

CHRIS CASSON MADDEN

Getaways

CAREFREE RETREATS *for* ALL SEASONS

Published by Clarkson N. Potter,
201 East 50th Street, New York, New York 10022.
Member of the Crown Publishing Group.

Random House, Inc.
New York, Toronto, London, Sydney, Auckland
www.randomhouse.com

CLARKSON N. POTTER, POTTER, and colophon
are registered trademarks of Random House, Inc.

Printed in the United States

Design by Douglas Turshen

Library of Congress Cataloging-in-Publication Data
Madden, Chris Casson.
    Getaways / Chris Casson Madden. — 1st ed.
    1. Vacation homes—United States. 2. Architecture,
Modern—20th century—United States. I. Title.
    NA7575.M14   2000
    728—dc21   99-24606
    CIP

ISBN 0-609-60320-5

10   9   8   7   6   5   4   3   2   1

First Edition

acknowledgments

WITH LOVE AND GRATITUDE to the men in my life: my husband, Kevin, who has written, edited, honed, and polished so much of this book, along with being "prop boy"; to Patrick, who truly understands the meaning of the word *getaway*; and to Nicky, who helped us discover our own getaway.

As always, I am grateful for the wisdom, understanding, and patience of my editor, Annetta Hanna. She is always there to guide me, encourage me, and, occasionally, gently prod me throughout these exhilarating but sometimes exhausting projects known as design books.

To my photographers, Jennifer Lévy and Nancy Hill, thank you for your great talents and for listening to me. I think that together we have created a stunning book. To Carolyn Schultz, who was there through many steps on the way, thanks!

The designer of *Getaways* is Doug Turshen. His talent is immense, his eye flawless. Thanks, Doug, for your insights and support. And to Nora Negron, for her hands-on design.

Special gratitude to everyone at Clarkson Potter. Barbara Marks always anticipates my questions and always has the right answers. Lauren Shakely and Chip Gibson, thank you for your support and guidance in this project, and my gratitude to all of your team at Clarkson Potter: Andy Martin, Joan DeMayo, Joan Denman, MarySarah Quinn, Lauren Monchik, Mark McCauslin, Camille Smith, Robin Strashun, Ari Gerson, John Son, Julie Zimmerman, and Christian Red.

To Bob Barnett and Jackie Davies at Williams & Connolly, thanks so much for your advice and for patiently answering all my questions.

I can't say enough about my assistants who have been involved in *Getaways*. To Kerry Christensen, for keeping cool under the pressure of our last-minute deadlines, thanks. And to Nannette Gonzales, my appreciation for all your efforts.

A special thanks to all those people who advised and encouraged me in the course of this project: Toni Morrison, Jennifer and James D'Auria, Sarah Smith, Bagley Reid, Justin and Lee Casson, Daphne DuPont, Electa Anderson, Christine Brooks, Karen Reisler, Mark Zeff, Diane Johnson, Sheri Schlesinger, Brenda Fox Wilson, Ron Lessard, John Hoppenthala, Kim Kimball, Marian McEvoy, David Lawrence Gray, Debra Wassman, Jonathan Lanman, Barbara Ross, Kathy Johnson, Karen Johnson, Frank Newbold, Mary Grace, and Frank Grace. I met so many people who were gracious and helpful to me during the creation of *Getaways*: Rob Fariel at the Sea Breeze Inn in Amagansett, Charles and Roe DiSapio at Country Gear in Bridgehampton, Lynn Ring at Executive Yacht Management in Marina Del Rey, Dave Viers at Montana Boot Company in Livingston, Daphne Fine in Saratoga Springs, Jan Diedrich at Homesteaders Furniture in Big Timber, Dave Taylor at Chico Hot Springs, and the very special people at Indigo Seas in Los Angeles, Roger's Gardens in Corona del Mar, and Mecox Gardens in Southampton. And to the countless others who helped me along the way, thanks!

contents

introduction

WHEN I TRAVELED AROUND THE COUNTRY TALKING TO
readers about my last book, *A Room of Her Own: Women's Personal Spaces,*
I was struck by how many women told me they had created—or
yearned to create—a personal space, a private sanctuary for themselves
in their homes. The concept of a personal space struck a deeply respon-
sive chord with so many women, which seemed to cut across all demo-
graphic boundaries—age, geography, whatever.

But as I talked to people, it also became increasingly clear to me
that the need for a haven, a retreat, is a universal one. Families, couples,
and singles—regardless of gender—share this almost primal urge to have
what began to take shape in my mind as a "getaway." Suddenly, and with
a sense of energizing enthusiasm, I was on to a new project—*Getaways.*

As I do with all my books, I got on the phone, sent out letters, and
faxed friends and designers asking them if they had or knew of a getaway, a special place that offered a sense of sanctuary. I was thrilled to
receive a huge and enthusiastic response to my queries. Some wrote
eloquently about their homes on the water, whether this was the ocean,
a lake, or a small harbor. Others submitted wonderful photographs of
shacks in the mountains or secluded cottages. I found that a getaway did
not have to be a second home: many had created one in their primary
home or apartment right in the midst of the city.

Toni Morrison, the Nobel Prize–winning author whose home I was
privileged to photograph, eloquently captured the essence of a getaway.
"It's a vision of a place you've had in your mind," Toni told me, "and
when you find yourself there, you recognize it." I discovered eye-pleasing
spaces that came in a dazzling variety of guises, from the Donahue

The discovery of a getaway, I found,

family's charming boat basin in Rye, New York (which has been in the family for three generations), to actor Michael Keaton's fishing shack in the Rockies to Los Angeles designer Lynn von Kersting's secluded pool and pavilion snuggled above the clamor of Sunset Boulevard. Katie Couric let me photograph her elegantly relaxed home in upstate New York, where she and her daughters escape on weekends from her hectic schedule at NBC. I traveled out to the end of eastern Long Island where Walter Iooss, Jr., the well-known sports photographer, and his wife Eva opened their incredible home to me on the Montauk cliffs overlooking the Atlantic Ocean.

A very talented designer, Sarah Smith, gave me and my photographer access to several exquisite getaways on a small island off the Connecticut coastline, where three or four generations of families gather each summer. The design philosophy there was very much one of relaxed comfort. Sand-filled Top-Siders and water-soaked golden retrievers were welcome in any room of the house!

The discovery of a getaway, I found, often has the characteristics of an epiphany. Renate McKnight and her artist-husband, Tom, owned homes in New York and Palm Beach but were visiting friends in bucolic Litchfield

often has the characteristics of an epiphany.

County in Connecticut when they drove past a stately old Colonial house on Litchfield's Main Street. As Tom told me, "We both knew it was the house we wanted." They contacted a local real estate agent and have now lovingly restored and renovated this wonderful home.

Jennifer and James D'Auria told me a similar tale about the discovery of their getaway. New Yorkers through the week, Jennifer is an actress and James an architect. They had a small weekend house on eastern Long Island but both had a very clear vision of the house and property they yearned for. One night, while driving in a wild rainstorm, Jennifer spotted a For Sale sign on a piece of land. As Jennifer said, "The country road was right, the hills were right." She drove back, got James, and, as you'll see, created an exquisite home in the potato fields of Amagansett.

Time and again, the owners of the spaces I photographed reiterated the sentiment that Toni Morrison had expressed to me, that feeling of "coming home." Whenever we find this place—whether at the beach, in the country, or in our everyday homes—I know that we can add a richness to our wondrous but sometimes hectic lives by following our vision and creating a getaway of our own.

reclaiming the past

harbor
hideaway

BAGLEY REID IS A TRANSPLANTED Southerner living on an island off the coast of New England. From his native Virginia he brought with him a discerning eye, a green thumb cultivated in a warmer clime, and a respect for land, property, and family ties that run deep.

As a young man, Bagley was a weekend houseguest on the island that has now become his home. In the early 1970s, he left behind an investment banking career in New York and made this bucolic island his main residence. A dockside oyster seed fishery, formerly a carpenter shop, caught Bagley's eye and captured his imagination. He set out to renovate it as a home for himself and his family.

"This building gets wonderful light," says Bagley. "When it was a carpenter shop, the entire 30-by-50-foot first floor was open space. The windows extend around the whole perimeter so the workers could use the natural light. I knew it would be a perfect space in which to raise my young sons and allow them to experience the unique joys of life on an island."

The exterior of the barn now has a true Scandinavian feel. Bagley designed the landscaping, and in the process he found a new calling. He planted the gardens and fruit trees that now flourish in the courtyard between the barn and an outbuilding, which has been converted into a greenhouse and shed.

For the renovation of the barn's interior, Bagley worked with a coterie of skilled carpenters from Vermont. They divided the first floor into a master bedroom and bathroom suite, a spacious, open living and dining room area, and a separate kitchen.

OPPOSITE: *Tucked under the eaves is a child-friendly sleeping alcove with a well-worn Berber carpet underneath.* ABOVE: *A ladder for an adventurous climber to reach the cupola, with its 360-degree views of the harbor and beyond, was constructed with a skylight window at the top.*

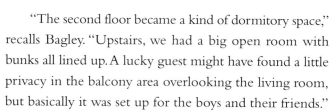

"The second floor became a kind of dormitory space," recalls Bagley. "Upstairs, we had a big open room with bunks all lined up. A lucky guest might have found a little privacy in the balcony area overlooking the living room, but basically it was set up for the boys and their friends."

With the harbor and a boatyard across the street, a short bicycle ride to the beach and tennis courts, and with friends and each other for playmates, Bagley's three sons had carefree summer experiences.

"Then they grew up and got married," says Bagley. "All of a sudden, the prospect of bringing their brides home to share a dormitory space wasn't so appealing. Since the boys still liked spending time here together, we decided it was time for another renovation."

This time, Bagley and his sons—with the talents of a carpenter from Charlottesville, Virginia—reconfigured the dorm space and created separate suites for each family unit.

"The house always was a joint family effort, although the renovations were 20 years apart. Each time the boys were an integral part of the work," Bagley says.

Realizing it would not be too long before his grandchildren would want their own space, Bagley constructed a cupola-cum-hideaway at the top of the barn. Designed for adventurous children and trim adults, the little loft space is reached by a narrow ladder that leads to a cozy bed nestled under a skylight. This small hideaway is always filled with books and pillows and a few toys—perfect accoutrements for a getaway.

peaceful solitude

WHEN THE TRAFFIC IS FLOWING smoothly, New York–based designer Mariette Himes Gomez can be in her weekend home in about one hour. She created her getaway about 15 years ago—moving the main barn and several outbuildings of an early nineteenth-century dairy farm to their present location in a fallow field in a Long Island farming community.

A high-profile, energetic designer, and a member of the Interior Design Hall of Fame, Mariette has a roster of international celebrity clients. She also designs a successful line of high-end furniture pieces, which are modern adaptations of classical forms. Many people are surprised that her second home is so dramatically different from her city life in both New York and London. To Mariette, the barns on her property are symbolic of both worlds. They represent "the opportunity to get out of the city to the quiet and solitude of the country," she explains, "yet they are still so close to Manhattan." While readying these buildings for human habitation, Mariette made sure that the barns' basic integrity was maintained. Simplicity and informality were inherent in the original design, so the conversion from barn to second home was a natural.

"My getaway here is about relaxing and doing the things I can't do in my very frenetic 'other' life," she says. "I like the peace and quiet. I come here for solitude. I read here; I've been working on watercolors and needlepoint. I come here whenever I can."

The main barn is the "family headquarters," while the outlying sheds are now a guest house and a pool house. "The guest house was a home for chickens 100 years ago," Mariette notes; originally she used it as a shed to

OPPOSITE: Softened by paint and light, a former chicken coop is transformed into a summer sanctuary. Mariette's collection of lighthouse paintings is the inspiration for the cottage's moniker.
ABOVE: Exposed sheathing adds some necessary shelving and panache to the cottage's bathroom.

ABOVE: *A stylish tableau for a summer weekend: a gingham satchel, a Panama hat, a beach mat, and a summer scene of Long Island when farms dominated the area.* OPPOSITE: *A potpourri of linen and embroidered hand towels beside a toile-covered chair.*

store extraneous lawn and garden equipment. "But it was an opportunity waiting to happen. It was in real need of repair—the shed needed some attention or it would have had to have been torn down."

Mariette and some friends were sitting by the pool one day, lamenting the shed's state of disrepair, when they dreamed up the idea to turn it into a guest cottage. "My good friends Donald Kaufman and Taffy Dahl encouraged me to convert it," confides Mariette. The results were in keeping with the rest of the buildings on the property, which she describes as "very informal, with a stylishly casual atmosphere."

There was no real structural redesign in transforming chicken coop to guest quarters. "It wasn't a renovation so much as a restoration. Except for adding a bath, we didn't modernize it. We really just put on a new roof, replaced the windows, added a floor, and whitewashed the interior," says Mariette. "I worked with George Kepczynski, a local craftsman based in Flanders, who helped me pull it together in record time. Now it's used by friends and relatives—guests who just want to be off by themselves and

ABOVE: *Whitewashed doors and window frames transform the former shack into a cozy summer retreat under a maple shade tree.*
OPPOSITE LEFT: *A hanging mirror in the front entry reflects the outdoors. An oak chest and two candlestick lamps finish the space.*

gather only for communal meals, a swim, or cocktails. Otherwise, they get to enjoy the solitude." Recently completed, the guest cottage completes the family compound of converted buildings.

Called the Lighthouse Cottage because of its collection of lighthouse paintings, it measures only 8 by 22 feet—offering a small but luxurious hideaway for guests. A crescent moon has been carved into its front door, and a large comfortable Adirondack chair outside is repeated in miniature inside. The whitewashed walls with their hooks and crossbeams create perfect storage and display areas. A slip of gingham fabric is transformed into a curtain, with Battenberg lace valances made from an old tablecloth. Two

It means so much when you find a place

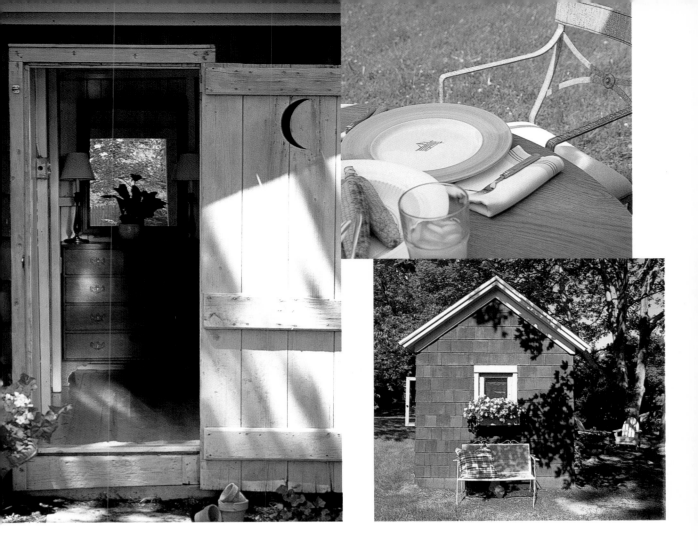

practical Hansen swing reading lamps, an overhead ceiling fan, Egyptian cotton linens, and a collection of soft bed pillows complete the sleeping area, while a tiny bathroom has been outfitted with both antiques and amenities for overnight visitors.

A swimming pool is the strongest clue that this former farm is now dedicated to more leisurely pursuits. Geraniums and ivy, irises and roses, bespeak an interest more in landscape and horticulture than in horses and husbandry. "This place is so peaceful—it means so much when you find a place where you can feel that sense of solitude—it certainly is a good anti-dote to the visibility and social routine of my other life."

TOP RIGHT: Set for lunch: one of four metal chairs that Mariette found in a local shop and the wooden hunt table. BOTTOM RIGHT: A vintage wrought-iron settee with madras pillow stylishly completes one end of the shed.

where you can feel that sense of solitude.

montauk restoration

THE MAIN HOUSE OF THE getaway compound of Manhattan architect Daniel Romualdez in Montauk, Long Island, was photographed by *House Beautiful* in 1957, before Daniel was even born. In that issue the magazine celebrated the small house for its heritage and thoughtful restoration, noting that some portions of the cottage were built in the 1760s, and that its Dutch-style, hand-hewn shingle construction was a monument to New England ingenuity updated for modern life.

Under Daniel's custodianship, the cedar-shingled house today bears little resemblance to its circa 1950s ambience. "When I bought the house from the previous owner, a doctor," he recalls, "I wanted to warm it up. I wanted to alter it from that Yankee Puritan aesthetic." With his skilled architect's touch, he has filled the house with his own eclectic and sophisticated collection of furniture, and has painstakingly unearthed original paint treatments, restoring the house to its indigenous cottage roots. This compound of three small dwellings and two terraces, one for dining and one for sunning and gazing, is perched high on the windblown dunes overlooking the Atlantic. The house originally had its own windmill and was located farther out on Long Island, near the Montauk Point lighthouse.

Moved to their present location in the 1970s, the cottages have made peace with the elements. With both New World and Old Dutch influences, they would look at home washed up on either shore of the Atlantic. They have been bleached and softened by their environment and have over the years acquired the patina of driftwood and shell, sand and sea grass.

The main house is sparsely decorated and edited with an eye toward

OPPOSITE: *The strong lines of an iron and leather bench are in sharp contrast to the Adirondack-style table.*
ABOVE: *Weathered cedar shingles and natural stone steps are essential and handsome elements in this Atlantic environment.*
OVERLEAF: *Plank pine floors support the mixture of periods, textures, and shapes in the dining room.*

ABOVE: *Polychromed doors, painted in the thirties, with a distinctively Eastern European influence, were uncovered during the reno-vation.* FAR LEFT: *Over a table from Niall Smith hangs a pyramid of natural history.* NEAR LEFT: *A still life composed on an antique marble-topped console table.* RIGHT: *A separate guest cottage contains an iron bed and original pine planking.*

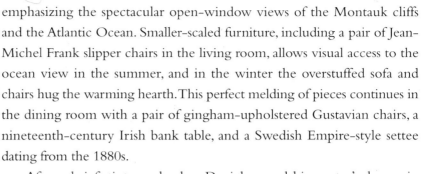

emphasizing the spectacular open-window views of the Montauk cliffs and the Atlantic Ocean. Smaller-scaled furniture, including a pair of Jean-Michel Frank slipper chairs in the living room, allows visual access to the ocean view in the summer, and in the winter the overstuffed sofa and chairs hug the warming hearth. This perfect melding of pieces continues in the dining room with a pair of gingham-upholstered Gustavian chairs, a nineteenth-century Irish bank table, and a Swedish Empire-style settee dating from the 1880s.

After a brief stint as a banker, Daniel earned his master's degree in architecture at Columbia School of Architecture. He worked for architect Robert A. M. Stern and designers Peter Marino and Thierry Despont; he also worked on projects with the renowned architecture critic Paul Goldberger. His firm, Daniel Romualdez Architects, P.C., is involved in wide-ranging design assignments throughout the country. With his hectic and engaged work schedule in Manhattan, he feels that it is very important for both him and his partner to find the time to regularly retreat to their Montauk sanctuary. "There is no fax or voice mail here. I purposely kept the telephone with a rotary dial," he says.

For Daniel this is an all-weather retreat. "In the summer," he says, "I love to fish and I'm really into kayaking. I paddle along the shore and am bounced along by the waves." He also ventures into these occasionally treacherous waters to bodysurf and wanders the rocky shore, hiking and beachcombing. "In the winter," he goes on, "we mountain bike or hang out in the house and make a stew; read or do cross-word puzzles in front of the fire, listening to the surf. It is so peaceful."

When he entertains in the warm weather, it is outdoors, where lunch is served on a 12-foot-long slate table situated under an arbor. "Once a month we invite friends to come by for lunch, hit the beach, and swim. It's very casual."

With its strong emphasis on comfort and simplicity, even the guest cottage—a stone's throw from the main house—echoes Daniel's relaxed preferences. "My friends argue over who gets to stay in the little cottage—they all say how magical it is. You feel like you're transported to another place."

BELOW LEFT: *Daniel on the rocky Montauk shore at the edge of the Atlantic Ocean.* BELOW RIGHT: *A late-afternoon stroll down the beach path from Daniel's house.*

ABOVE: *A cool conversational area on the slate terrace, with the surf as ever-present background music.*

Friends come by for lunch, hit the

BELOW LEFT: *The Dutch front door.* BELOW RIGHT: *The main house sits high on a cliff, surrounded by wildflowers. The original screen and wooden doors and shutters are naturally distressed—a pleasing combination with the weather-beaten gray shingles of the house.*

ABOVE LEFT: *A summer salad of well-seasoned fresh tomatoes and basil on the al fresco dining table.* ABOVE RIGHT: *A ready bar after a full day of fishing, set up in the back entrance to the house.*

beach, and swim; it's very casual.

perfect
partners

HERE BEGINS THE STORY OF
an odd marriage with a fairy-tale
ending. A New England spinster
of gentle breeding and good man-
ners marries a lonely, hardworking bachelor farmer from New Hampshire.
She is elegance personified, slight of stature but perfect in proportion; her
face is pale and unlined. He is rough and coarse, big-boned and sturdy, and
the years and weather have left their etchings on his skin.

Their education and backgrounds couldn't be more dissimilar. But
what they have in common is an honest, simple outlook on life. Practical as
salt, these two know what it is to maintain their own values and persevere
through a long, lonely life.

They meet in the most old-fashioned of ways, through a marriage
broker of sorts; a person who knows instinctively when two are perfect for
each other. Without family or inheritance, they're free to take the advice of
the broker, end their loneliness, and marry, sight unseen.

Never was a marriage so idyllic. The broker helped them in the honeymoon phase to negotiate the discrepancies in their heritages and person-
alities. Now they have made the most of their late-in-life marriage and have
settled on an island. They are living out the rest of their lives in grace and
modest elegance, offering hospitality and refuge to newfound family and
friends, surrounded by the raw beauty and energy of the Atlantic Ocean.

The marriage broker in this story is BD Remodeling and Restoration,
a company based on an island off the Connecticut coast. Dave Beckwith is
an expert in restoration, woodcraft, and stonemasonry. He found two
structures: one a circa 1830 New England Greek Revival house, and the
other a New Hampshire corncrib built in 1860.

OPPOSITE: *A tabletop display—a combination of the rustic and the refined.* ABOVE: *A hand-hewn chair catches the afternoon sunlight.* OVERLEAF: *Furnishings in the corncrib living room are eclectic. A Shaker chair combines with wicker and pine, making this room pleasing to the eye. A sturdy staircase leads to the master bedroom above.*

OPPOSITE: *The master bedroom
is tucked under the eaves
above the living room. A dramatic
black needlepoint rug is in
sharp contrast to the pine planks
of the old corncrib, while windows
offer a stunning water view.*

Dave called his business partner, who agreed to the purchases of the structures and found the land on which to situate the buildings for the perfect marriage. It all happened very quickly and was transacted in a very modern way, by cell phone, closing deals and buying land almost sight unseen. But Dave knows a bargain when he sees one: the Greek Revival portion of the finished house was purchased for five hundred dollars in 1994.

The bones of the house were good and the restoration didn't require any structural changes, so "everything is exactly the same, only now the windows aren't broken and it's painted," says Dave.

What he doesn't elaborate on is how the house was moved board by board, loaded in sections onto an island ferry, and reconstructed on the site. It was united to its corncrib partner, now the main living room and master bedroom of the house, by a connecting galley kitchen.

How long did this marriage take? "About twelve months; we were held up because an archeological dig for Indian remains on our new land had to be completed before the reconstruction could begin," remembers Dave.

Then the corncrib portion had to be modified for human habitation without changing the layout and feel of its original interior. "The only things we added to the corncrib were the Palladian-style windows and the stone fireplace. Everything else—the electric system, pipes, air-conditioning, and heat ducts—was applied to the exterior of the 'barn.' We then put an old barn-board shell on top of that. It's called the 'envelope style' of reconstruction," says Dave.

The honeymoon is just beginning, and the final house does indeed represent the perfect marriage. "I love this house," Dave says. "I love the contrast of opposites, the simplicity and the elegance, the rough and the refined."

BELOW: *The slender columns of the Greek Revival porch stand sentry over a much-loved and well-used portion of the home. Wicker furniture with green-and-white awning-stripe cushions and floral accent pillows dress up the porch for summer entertaining. The swimming pool beckons in the background.*

ABOVE: *Sage green kitchen cabinets ease the transition between the two old structures.* ABOVE RIGHT: *A collection of sea glass catches the light in an antique biscuit jar in the living room.*

The contrasts of opposites: the

BELOW: *Festive red, white, and blue bunting hangs over the main road of the island.*

ABOVE: *An exterior view of the happy melding of the old corncrib and the Greek Revival house. The graceful window offers a peek through to the back.*
ABOVE RIGHT: *The view from the master bedroom. Old pilings mark the site of a former dock.*

simple and the elegant, the rough and refined.

cliff
dwellers

THE TOWERING CLIFFS overlooking the Atlantic Ocean in Montauk, on the eastern end of Long Island, are a visual jolt to first-time visitors to this storied seaside town. The surrounding villages of East Hampton and Amagansett, notable for their gently rolling dunes and soil-rich farm fields, stand in stark contrast to Montauk's dramatic cliffs.

Eva and Walter Iooss, Jr., first bought a cozy, run-down weekend cottage in Montauk in 1977. Eva, a former model and now a decorative artist, and Walter, a renowned sports photographer, were already in love with Montauk and wanted to build a getaway there. As Eva recalls, "We loved to walk on the cliffs and it was our dream to build a home on them. Walter called a realtor who told us about this land right next to the Seven Sisters—seven beautiful Stanford White summer cottages. We went to the site—which was forested—and climbed a tree to see the view. It was love at first sight! We could see the water and hear the surf. We bought the land in 1980."

Working with the architectural team of Tony Tyson and Michael Geyer, Eva and Walter designed and built a traditional Shaker shingle-style house with a peaked roof, and, as Eva notes, "with fireplaces everywhere." In 1988, a structure—originally built as Walter's workspace and an occasional guest house—was added and eventually became Eva's studio, where she goes to create botanical paintings in oil and watercolor.

A garden, thick and lush, stands in front of the main cottage facing the ocean. The lawn slopes gently down to a large hedge and a stone wall that gives the yard a sense of enclosure and serves as a buffer against the cold

OPPOSITE: *A display of Eva's botanical works-in-progress creates a stunning still life: a weathered table, paint tools, and a tray of collected butterfly specimens.* ABOVE: *Built originally for Walter's photography, the studio subsequently became a guest cottage and has evolved into a painting studio for Eva.*

RIGHT: *Eva selects the proper brush for her work at the easel. A decorative painter, she now specializes in botanicals.* BELOW: *Several of Eva's colorful working palettes in her easel tray.*

RIGHT: *An early work of Eva's, a reclining nude, hangs on the back wall. A current project rests on the easel next to an old Victorian kitchen chair, which serves as a painter's stool.* OPPOSITE: *A close-up of Eva's worktable and the tools of her trade: paints, brushes, and some touches of inspiration.*

ABOVE: *An ocean fog softly veils the shrubs planted along the top of the cliff overlooking the Atlantic. A wall of double French doors opens up the studio to the adjacent porch and the sweeping lawn below.*

winds of early spring and late fall. A separate garden provides summer bounty; its varied specimens serve as the models for the exacting botanicals that Eva renders. Originally from the Netherlands, Eva feels the land here is evocative of Holland and Ireland. "My heart totally skipped a beat when I first saw Montauk, with its coves, rocky beaches, high dunes, cliffs, ponds, and inland waterways—it was all very Dutch-looking," she says.

Walter's illustrious career—he is one of *Sports Illustrated*'s premier photographers and a chronicler of Michael Jordan's career—takes him around the world on assignments, but every weekend, and for longer periods in the summer, he and Eva and their two sons, Christian and Björn, escape to Montauk from their home in the Riverdale neighborhood of New York City. Walter says, "The ocean is the big lure—it's the pulse of life, it's in our veins. We love the freedom, the space, and the friends we have here."

"I'm religious about driving out here every weekend," notes Eva. "I've

driven through snowstorms and near-hurricane conditions to get here. This is where our heart is." Like the neighboring historic houses on the Montauk cliffs, the Iooss house has stood the test of major storms. "The house shakes," recalls Eva, "and the trees bend down so far they almost hit the grass. We've had tree damage but we know the house is solid. Walter and I believe it could survive winds up to 150 miles per hour."

Family activities include strolling down the paths to the cove below, collecting rocks, and perhaps the most popular pull, surfing, especially before and after storms. "Here you are, bobbing in the water in the middle of a place you love most. You see things differently than from land," notes Walter. Adds Eva, "We also play volleyball with friends on the lawn every couple of weeks. Everyone brings a dish and my little garden is all set up with food and a bar. The gazebo is lit up with a soft yellow light. It's magical and we love it!"

TOP LEFT: *A windmill motif on the wooden gate pays homage to Eva's Dutch heritage.* TOP RIGHT: *Eva returning home from the local nursery.* BOTTOM LEFT: *A page of old text is enlivened with painted jonquils.* BOTTOM RIGHT: *Walter and Eva with sons Christian and Björn on the porch.*

family ties

country
treasure

WE ALL KNOW WHERE TO FIND
Katie Couric on weekdays. For
two hours each morning we can
follow her from inside the NBC
studios at "30 Rock" to outside
on the street, rain or shine. There
she mingles with Matt Lauer and
Al Roker and the hundreds of spirited New Yorkers and waving tourists
who throng the famous plaza, bearing placards and sporting T-shirts that
identify them as members of such-and-such high school band or drama
club. So much activity—and all before most of us have had our first cup of
coffee! It's little wonder that Katie needs an escape come the weekend.
With relief and a sigh, she and her two children head for the green meadows and rolling hills of Dutchess County, New York.

"We decided on Dutchess County because it reminded us of Virginia,"
explains Katie, who grew up in Virginia and graduated with honors from
that state's university, founded by Thomas Jefferson. Set up on a hill, her
house overlooks a picturesque hamlet. The sweeping lawn, stone fences,
and white church and steeple across the lane resemble the country settings
where James Stewart and Katharine Hepburn frolicked in *The Philadelphia
Story,* or where Barbara Stanwyck and Dennis Morgan flirted in *Christmas
in Connecticut.*

"A lot of the houses were really isolated," says Katie. "We liked this one
because it is private but without the feeling of total isolation I got from
other places we looked at. There is a sense of living in a neighborhood."

The presence of Katie's late husband is evident in every room. Jay
Monahan chose much of the furnishings and had considerable input in

*OPPOSITE: A side table
displays a grouping of
family photos and is
flanked by a collection of
antique walking sticks.
The mirror was a gift
from Katie's mother-in-
law.* ABOVE: *An early-
morning moment in
the tree-shaded garden.*

PRECEDING PAGES: *Plush upholstered furniture in a rose-and-cream toile anchors the music room. Nineteenth-century chairs from a church in Virginia stand on either side of the marble fireplace.* RIGHT: *Katie's collection of antique pillboxes from her grandmother.* BELOW: *Life in the country includes the childhood piano Katie brought with her from Virginia.*

OPPOSITE: *In the corridor connecting the music room to the study, an antique reversible bench rests under oil paintings collected by Katie and Jay.*

the decorating. The interiors are relaxed—not at all fussy. Though there are lots of toys, thanks to their young daughters, Ellie and Carrie, the feel of the house is very much that of a Southern gentleman's. In the music room, walking sticks, country furniture, rare books, and historic paintings dominate. Several pieces from Jay's collection of Civil War memorabilia are on display.

The centerpiece of the music room is the old Cable upright piano. "I grew up with it," says Katie. "It's the one I learned to play on, so it's nice that the girls can learn to play on it, too." In keeping with the sentiment of the heirloom instrument, it is crowned with a collection of photographs of family, friends, and special occasions.

The furniture in the music room also has important family significance. "Jay's mother gave us the gold mirror and my parents bought the sideboard beneath it at an estate sale," Katie says. "Jay and I picked out the covered bench that stands in front of the fireplace at an antique store in Hudson, New York."

ABOVE: *The surrounding fields and fences reminded Katie and Jay of the rolling hills of the horse country in Virginia. A garden plot is cultivated in a pasture near the carriage house.*

The original fireplace mantel was reinstalled against the hand-rubbed finish of terra-cotta walls, which created a warm backdrop for the piece. Antique English treens—drinking cups turned by young boys learning the art of woodcrafting—are arranged on the mantel. Katie picked out the Cowtan & Tout fabric used on most of the furniture while Jay chose the rug, and they both selected the oil painting from Scotland that hangs above the fireplace. Decorating the room was very much a family affair.

The Greek Revival house, built circa 1820, did not require much structural change when Katie moved in. With the help of Jonathan Lanman and Debra Wassman of Trumbull Architects, "we redid the kitchen, built baths out of closets, and turned a bath into a guest room—not major changes. We did mostly decorating," says Katie. A friend and designer, Karen Reisler, also helped Katie and Jay in this effort.

What Katie appreciates most about her country home is that "the kids can run around in a big yard and do all the things we used to do growing

up. We eat breakfast outside, the kids play with their toys out here, they read, and do puzzles." Eldest daughter Ellie adds, "We can climb trees and I can go outside in my pajamas!"

Katie and the girls swim, pick vegetables and flowers from the garden, and do numerous craft projects together. Katie and Ellie have recently been experimenting with mosaics, decoupage, and Popsicle stick art, and they love entertaining Carrie with "homemade" balloons from a kit Katie picked up in London. Summer is outdoor time, but she and the girls also enjoy ice-skating in winter and have become "champion bowlers," Katie says, laughing.

In short, Katie's retreat is focused on her children and enjoying her time with them. "This was Jay's dream house—a place where we could all come and be happy and relaxed," she reflects. "This house gives us lots of privacy and makes me feel like I'm worlds away from my New York life." And that, after all, is what a getaway is all about.

ABOVE LEFT: *Ellie enjoys the swing before breakfast.* TOP: *From the side lawn, a view of the stone terrace: a shady setting for summer lunches and family games.* ABOVE: *Katie and the girls in the vegetable garden.* OVERLEAF: *A stone rooster keeps watch over the entrance to the early-nineteenth-century home.*

This house makes me feel like I'm

worlds away from my New York life.

island
traditions

LIKE BIRDS RETURNING TO the same nesting grounds year after year, people who were lucky enough to summer on an island as children can't help but feel that part of them is programmed to return to that island every summer for the rest of their lives. This is true even as the familial group grows ever larger, as children get married and produce children of their own.

Some families respond to this phenomenon by creating a compound of homes—little cottages connected by paths that allow several generations to coexist on a single property. Others respond as the owners of this house on a New England island have, by piecing together a house like parts of a puzzle—adding, modifying, and restoring—to build a compound under one roof, complete with separate living quarters for three generations, but with large enough communal spaces in which to cook, dine, and enjoy the outdoors together.

"This is a great family house," explains the owner, a woman who has summered on this island since her children were small. "Every generation has their own sitting area and bath, and the porch is our outdoor family room. It's such a solid house that we can all live here side by side."

Built in 1928, the house is backed by the porch, which extends the length of the traditional shingle-style home. It adjoins a pool looking out over the ocean and serves the function of dining room, sitting room, garden, and recreation room. It is also the main gathering spot of the island's Fourth of July party, when up to 350 guests gather to toast and celebrate the birth of a nation.

OPPOSITE: A welcoming view from the front door allows visitors a framed perspective of the foyer, living room, and porch to the ocean beyond.
ABOVE: Inside the foyer an antique painted tallboy holds emblems of Americana beside a peripatetic collection of walking sticks.

ABOVE: *The spacious
foyer anchored by a
circular pedestal table
affords easy access to
the living room on the
left, the stairs to the
master bedroom above,
and the billiard room/
library below.*
OPPOSITE: *Sumptuous
fabrics and American
antiques create a
romantically relaxed
living room.*

The owners of this home did extensive renovations to make it more commodious and relaxed for their family. They redesigned the foyer to open it up to the view of the grays and blues of the Atlantic Ocean. "In the past, you walked in and saw a fireplace wall," says the owner. "I wanted to make it so that one immediately sees the water upon entering our home."

Islands encourage relaxation, but, she continues, "I love the process of renovation, I love the sawdust. Finding the craftsmen and watching them at their work is especially energizing," she says. "The caliber of the crafts-people who restore the architectural details, such as the mantel, and who match the old woods to such expert degree that you can't tell where the old ends and the new begins is always enormously gratifying to me."

Summer and especially the holidays are family time on the island. "This place is more home to my kids than our house on the mainland," explains the owner. "Here on this island, life slows down. It is a restful, much less serious place. When the phone rings, it's usually 'What time do you want to play tennis?'" They wanted to establish the island's slower pace as a summer routine for their children and grandchildren, and the house itself reflects this philosophy.

OPPOSITE: *In the sitting room outside the master bedroom, a nineteenth-century pine secretary houses a collection of early American baskets and letter holders.*
RIGHT: *In the library, an old needlepoint commemorates the man who "was talked to death." A standing Chinese-style painted lamp and a Windsor chair are some examples of the fine antiques found throughout the house.*

ABOVE: *A library ladder for the floor-to-ceiling bookcase keeps the reading material accessible to everyone in the house.* RIGHT: *A pool table adds a sporting note to the lower-level library, while an arched doorway allows a peek into the living room.*

BELOW LEFT: *The kitchen is perfect for casual meals. The iron stars that are found in old buildings are a favorite collectible.* BELOW RIGHT: *Stars and stripes are an ever-present motif in this house, where the Fourth of July is an enthusiastically celebrated holiday.*

Here on this island, life slows down;

BELOW: *The porch is the outdoor family room, spacious enough for three generations to gather and enjoy the view and each other. An antique fishing sign hangs from the ceiling, and a fan keeps the breezes stirred.*

ABOVE: *Two members of the family relax by the end of the pool, which is separated from the bay by a fragrant rose hedge. Striped market umbrellas provide welcome shade, while lightweight chaises are easily regrouped beside the pool.*

it is a restful, much less serious place.

highland
serenity

THE IDEA OF AN ISLAND HOME often conjures up the image of a ramshackle structure: charming but sometimes musty, sparsely decorated, and, in all likelihood, unheated. On the contrary, this rambling and comfortably elegant home on an island off the coast of New England is suggestive of a prosperous English country house. A New York couple—he a lawyer, she a travel agent—gather here most weekends, often joined by their grown children and their young grandchildren.

"We love this house and come here year-round," says one of the owners, who summered on the island as a child. "Even though it is our weekend house, we really consider this our true home."

Sarah Smith is the interior designer who helped restore this circa 1928 country house to its former glory. "I loved working on the house," says Sarah. "This is a family house the way it should be. The couple who own it are both very busy during the week with their careers, but come the weekend, three generations gather here. Everybody pitches in to cook, there are great places to curl up with a book, there's lovely scenery to inspire long walks, and, since this is an island, somebody's always out sailing!"

The long drive up to the house is laid out like a classic English estate park. Verdant gardens and groves of trees—birch, pine, and oak—dot the property, while the serene blue waters of Long Island Sound are visible over the garden hedge.

Sarah worked closely with the owners to create the ambience of a comfortable English country home. "The family had an attic full of

OPPOSITE: *In the small card room, an old European postal notice board filled with family photos and postcards overlooks a spirited poker game in progress.* ABOVE: *A hand-painted canvas floorcloth continues the card motif beneath the leather-tooled card table.*

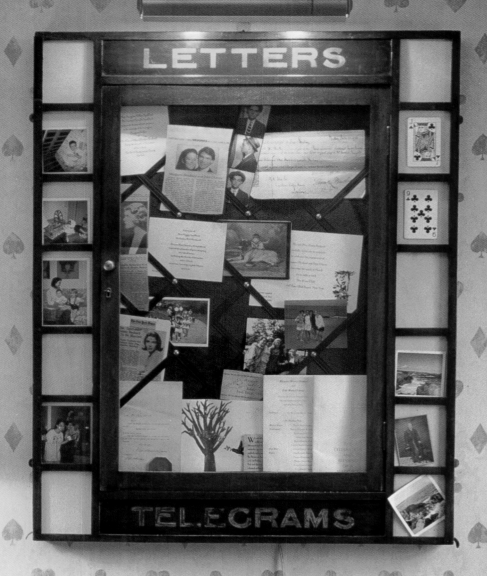

PRECEDING PAGES:
*Hand-painted lamp-
shades pick up the blues
and reds in the serape
carpet, while the lamps
cast a warm glow on the
original pine paneling in
the family living room.
A cozy fire makes this a
natural gathering spot
during family holidays
celebrated on the island.*
ABOVE: *Sherry served
in cranberry glass goblets
adds to the spirit of holiday warmth and cheer.*

antiques, so we had these pieces restored to furnish the rooms. They suggested the Old World country look," explains Sarah. The richly paneled
pine walls of the living room are original to the house and can hold their
own against the vibrant colors—blues predominate—of the oversized
antique serape carpet. The room has been zoned into two conversation
areas and the cozy array of furniture, with its collections of books, porcelains, paintings, and colored glass, reinforces the manor house mood. Many
of the details in the room are custom-designed or hand-painted. The love
seat, covered in a Brunschwig & Fils fabric, was designed by Sarah. The
symmetrical lamps on either side of the fireplace have lampshades hand-
painted by Emilie Henry to coordinate with the carpet and to bring out
the blues and reds in the room. Two Victorian slipper chairs, covered in a
pale cream and blue toile, and a ladder-back rocker complete the grouping.

A small card room off the living room is the scene of spirited multi-

generational card games; it is decorated with Osborne & Little wallpaper, a vintage card table, and a generous assortment of well-read books. The floorcloth—a painted canvas—was designed from an antique playing card by artist Elizabeth Gourlay. "We selected the king of hearts as befitting the lord of the manor," laughs Sarah. An old European postal notice board holds center stage as a gathering spot for family photographs and mementos.

Upstairs there are plenty of bedrooms for parents, children, and grand-children, each having staked their claim to a special spot. A family game room, complete with player piano, Ping-Pong table, and shelves of books and games, is a favorite spot on wet or snowy days.

This island getaway holds a special allure for its owners. On occasion, a fogged-in airport or canceled ferryboat can delay their arrival but, once there, the salty air, the windblown beach, and the weather-defying house make the trip all the more satisfying and worthwhile.

ABOVE LEFT: *An antique mantel clock, books, and old photos line the shelves in the card room.* TOP RIGHT: *An idyllic country bedroom for a young girl under the wallpapered eaves of the attic.* ABOVE: *An ivy-covered facade suggests the manor home of a traditional English estate.*

eternal weekends

WHEN JACQUELINE DEDELL met and married her husband, Ira, she says, "we both had enough life experience to know what we wanted." And what they wanted was something far away from the concrete of Manhattan. "We were focused on being somewhere outside of New York City," says Jackie.

Fortunately for both of them, they had jobs that could be managed by phone and fax just about anywhere as long as they occasionally put in some "face time" in at their offices in Manhattan. Jackie is the owner of Smashing Plates, a company that designs and manufactures ceramics and tabletop objects. Ira has a publishing company that sells visual and graphic books and CD-ROMs to the advertising trade.

As Ira explains it, "I was never a weekend-type person. The life that New Yorkers put up with—it's too wrenching. We wanted to live where we wanted to weekend. It was important for us to have the constant experience. We felt we were missing too many sunsets."

OPPOSITE: *Shetland ponies—pintos, bays, palominos, and chestnuts—are all part of the landscape at this working pony farm.* ABOVE: *The classic eighteenth-century farmhouse, lovingly restored and judiciously expanded, is reflected in the backyard pond. Geese landing on the pond inspired the name of the farm.*

So, Jackie and Ira, along with their young children, Skylar and Gavin, two dogs, numerous cats, a collection of parakeets and parrots, geese, chickens, goats, sheep, horses, bunnies, and ponies (lots of ponies), have established themselves on a working farm equipped with all the amenities of a weekend retreat—sunny breakfast room, outdoor pool, pond, and meadows—called "Goose Landing Farm," in Litchfield, Connecticut. They made a life here for themselves, their children, and the animals—an idyllic getaway.

They didn't achieve this overnight, nor did they do it alone. "We are both skilled at delegating," confesses Ira, and at dividing and conquering. They hired an extremely competent farm manager named Wendy Mur-

They made **an idyllic life** here for

themselves, their children, and the animals.

dock, who with help from her husband, Russ, and daughter, Christina, tends to all those ponies and farm animals, and helps in the weekend activities by organizing "fun drives" of horses and carriages, ponies and carts, attended by members of the local riding clubs.

With all the help, Ira and Jackie have had time to concentrate on fulfilling their dreams—raising and breeding ponies and sheep, horseback riding, hunting, learning how to make and sell goat cheese, and allowing their children to be raised with an appreciation of the entire birth-to-death process so evident in the countryside.

"For us and for our children, animals are such an important part of the whole experience. They've seen me give mouth-to-mouth resuscitation to a pony, for instance," says Ira. "We like being rural. I muck the stalls, I shovel the snow, but I also want to be able to go out and get a cup of cappuccino." And where they've established themselves in Connecticut, they've

got it all. "We love the sense of community—the mix of people and how we socialize and work together to achieve goals," adds Jackie.

Despite the cell phones and faxes, computers and E-mail, Jackie and Ira have a very traditional sense of the value of country life, and that is reflected throughout their house and property. The house was built in 1774. They added on a modern kitchen, greenhouse, and dining area, and updated the various work spaces around the farm. A corner of the kitchen contains a screened-in, oversized aviary that offers its own life cycle of nesting and birthing.

A pond surrounded by casual groupings of sturdy perennials makes the view from the breakfast room lovely year-round. "We're lucky," says Jackie. "Each season has its own part in the life cycle to be played out and here we can experience it all." Without interruption, weekends happen all week long at Goose Landing Farm.

TOP LEFT: *The author with Jackie, her husband, Ira, and children, Skylar and Gavin.* TOP RIGHT: *Gavin putting on a makeshift green behind the garden.* BOTTOM LEFT: *Some waddling namesakes of the farm.* BOTTOM RIGHT: *Ira and Gavin preparing for a drive with members of the local riding club.*

mountain roads

river's edge

TO MANY OF US, MICHAEL Keaton may be known for his somewhat frenetic comic roles—Beetlejuice, Dogberry in *Much Ado About Nothing*—or for his darker, more romantic portrayals—Batman, Bob Jones in *My Life*. But in the wide-open spaces of the former wild west, Michael is known as a rancher, builder, rider, skier, and just a "great guy."

Michael moved to this territory about five years ago. The congestion of Los Angeles is relieved for him by a vast landscape that rolls, builds momentum, and pushes itself into snow-covered peaks. In the approach to his remote western ranch, one can't help humming the tune "Give me land, lots of land under starry skies above, don't fence me in." For first-time visitors, the scene is evocative of the backdrops of the great Hollywood westerns of the forties and fifties.

When Michael first realized his dream and purchased land for his ranch, he spent time under the starry skies in a sleeping bag and in the back of a pick-up truck trying to find the perfect building sites. For the small fishing cabin not far from the main ranch house, he turned to local builder Terry Baird, who specializes in the restoration of old buildings. Baird found a centuries-old homesteader's cabin on another property and suggested to Michael that it would offer "perfect, basic living." The actor agreed and the two of them rebuilt the cabin with the help of architect Durward Sobek, who added a bathroom and porch to the humble log home.

Reassembled beside the banks of the river, amid a grove of shady birch

OPPOSITE: *The living room's relaxed furniture is enlivened with the vibrant colors from antique textiles. A Native American beaded ceremonial horse blanket adorns the coffee table, and pillows covered in rawhide rest on the sofa.*
ABOVE: *A view of the ranch as seen from the river.*

ABOVE: *Dandelions and meadow
grasses in a woven vase on
the bedside table in the sleeping
loft. Historical prints depict
the surrounding countryside.*
LEFT: *An old Naugahyde chair
is draped with a beacon
blanket and a southwestern-motif
pillow. A pioneer-made pine
cupboard holds dishes and collectibles in the kitchen beyond.*
RIGHT: *In the upstairs sleeping
loft, the cowboy vernacular
reigns. An old beacon blanket
makes the transition from
bunkhouse to bedroom where a
metal reading lamp is the
only suggestion of modernity.*

and aspen, the cabin fits Michael's need for simplicity and respite from the
Hollywood whirlwind. In late spring, he brings his horses from California
with him to summer at the ranch.

Michael approached designer Helen Kent and asked for her help in fur-
nishing the cabin. She shopped local antiques stores to put together its eclectic furniture, which includes two old Naugahyde easy chairs, a punched-tin
pie safe, an old pine kitchen table and hutch, a vintage writing table, and
twig porch furniture. Michael's collection of old beacon blankets, Navajo
rugs and textiles, and Native American artifacts add a layer of verve and
warmth to the sturdy and venerable homesteader's cabin.

ABOVE: *The strong log walls*
are an ever-present reminder of this
cabin's homesteading roots. Tucked into
the corner of the living room is an
antique drop-front writing desk from
a local antique shop.

The cabin fits Michael's need for

BELOW: *The original cabin was enhanced from its homesteading days with the addition of a front porch and a bumped-out sleeping loft.* RIGHT: *A kitchen porch, complete with Michael's fire-fighting gear, was added during the restoration and offers a great overlook of the river that runs through the property.*

ABOVE LEFT: *A found object—an elk's skull—rests alongside the cabin wall.* ABOVE: *A palomino finds refuge and sustenance in the flower-covered meadow.*

a respite from the Hollywood whirlwind.

hudson
pavilion

IN THE UPPER REACHES OF
the Hudson River valley, architect Steve Mensch has created a
compound that attempts to sat-
isfy the emotional, spiritual, and
practical needs of the people in
his life—and completely succeeds. The property includes a separate house
for his four teenage sons, a music studio for his pianist wife, Pam, and a
barn and animal shelter for his partner, landscape designer Greg Patnaude.
He designed a living space for all of them to share—to relax, read, and dine
in together—as well as a separate studio for his own artistic endeavors.

The grouping of buildings is situated on 22 acres about two hours
from New York City. Greg is largely responsible for the parklike aspects of
the property, which encompasses water-lily ponds, swan-inhabited lakes,
intimate paths, architectural expanses of bridges, colorful plantings, shady
groves, scenic vistas, and, original to the property, a roaring waterfall.

It is the waterfall that is the most notable feature of this extraordinary
property. Steve says that when he first encountered it, "it was a heart-
stopping gigantic sculpture, roaring with the waters of the melting snow. I
felt as if I was somewhere on the Rhine and immediately imagined a
modern version of one of crazy King Ludwig's castles.

"Watching the changing mood of the land as the snow and ice disap-
peared and the first gentle growth of spring emerged," Steve recalls, he
began to appreciate the incredible requirements necessary to construct a
house on such a site, literally at the apex of the falls. He wanted to create a
house inspired by the force and drama of the waterfall that would become
an organic unit, melding into this dramatic landscape. As he explains, "I

*OPPOSITE: The first
floor of Steve's
studio is devoted to his
architectural design
projects. A Mario Bellini
chair is at his clean-
lined desk, which looks
out onto the base of
the falls.* ABOVE: *Steve
perched on the ledge
in his studio's third-floor
bathing retreat.*

ABOVE: *Afternoon sunlight streaks across the family quarters, where sliding glass walls make open-air pavilions of the living and dining rooms, eliminating the barriers to the grounds and the falls beyond. A flagstone path leads out to a sitting area at the top of the falls.*

didn't want to hit it with one large building, but rather to go in as lightly as possible, seeking out places from which various aspects of the site could be appreciated, fitting small buildings carefully among the trees and into the contours, and placing the main public spaces at the waterfall."

Steve's final design plan featured five separate buildings—the main house; music studio; children's house; art and architecture studio; and a building for greenhouse use, storage, and garage; as well as several smaller open-air pavilions situated to capture various views of the falls.

The main house includes a copper-roofed glass pavilion that sits atop the three-story concrete structure. The concrete base of the main house has two levels for bedrooms and one for a screening room. The entire house is adjacent to the dam and the 50-foot waterfall, with the living room sharing the same plane as the top of the falls. One remarkable aspect of the living room area, aside from the surrounding views and nature, is that the glass walls fit into pockets, rendering them completely invisible, so that

LEFT: *The view from the window offers a serene backdrop for a marble Buddha that dates from the eleventh century.* BELOW: *Bath, banquette, and books on the third floor of the treehouse studio create Steve's private retreat overlooking the falls.*

LEFT: *Silk pillows on the low built-in seating offer a stroke of color in the artfully spare layout.* ABOVE: *A portal window offers a bird's-eye view.*

ABOVE: *Suggestive of Asian temples—
the family pavilion and one of several pagodas
in the "park" with the lush fall landscape
as backdrop. This view is made accessible by
crossing the suspension bridge at the top
of the property.* LEFT: *The red door of Steve's
studio is reached by a bridge constructed
between two trees left standing as sculptural
elements.* OPPOSITE: *Steve's three-story
structure on stilts houses his architectural and
painting studios and his bathing retreat.*

when the glass doors are slid back you are in the open air.

Shimmery silk pillows and an Oriental rug match the vibrancy of the fall colors outdoors, as does an earth-toned mural surround painted by Steve. Other items of household paraphernalia, including cooking and kitchen gear, are stored behind Honduran mahogany paneled closets and cupboards built flush with the walls. Mahogany paneling completes the interior walls and ceiling, and the floors are of unpolished black granite. Steve chose the stone because, he says, "I wanted radiant heat in the floors. The rugged beauty of the granite combines with the mahogany to create a quiet, contemplative mood." Each space in the Mensch compound is inextricably linked to the dramatic setting that surrounds it.

side hill farm

SIDE HILL FARM IS APTLY named. The house and barns that make up the country retreat of Maynard and Kay Toll and their three grown children have stood nestled on the western slope of this mountain in the Catskills range for over 150 years. Once a dairy farm, it is now the weekend destination for the Tolls and their friends. With hills for hiking and snowshoeing, a pond for fly-fishing, swimming, canoeing, and ice-skating, an outdoor Adirondack-style porch for shady relaxation, picnics, and spectacular mountain views and sunsets, the farm is the perfect spot to enjoy nature and outdoor activities year-round.

"We bought the property about 15 years ago when our kids were teenagers and just starting high school," says Kay. "Our friends all told us not to expect the kids to like this place. It was so remote, and now that they had all gone off to school, Maynard and I thought it would just be our special place. But instead, the kids fell in love with it. They all brought their friends. They loved it as much as we did, and we soon realized we would have to add quarters for the kids and all their friends."

The Tolls had the former heifer barn moved closer to the main house, and then transformed it into spacious guest quarters complete with a stone fireplace, an ample kitchen, and an authentic Japanese bath. Six years of living in Japan inspired the Tolls to add the bath to the guest house, which overlooks a rolling meadow. The peace and calm inherent in this ancient bathing ritual have further enhanced the sense of escape experienced at Side Hill Farm.

The Tolls were given the name of Sam Takenuchi, who specialized in

OPPOSITE: *The layering textures of the Side Hill Farm tub and its surround: warm tile, rough stone, smooth, polished bamboo flooring, and feather-light cotton robes on an antique ladder.* ABOVE: *Soaps in a soapstone bowl for the cleansing ritual before entering the bath.*

The porch evolved from necessity and

turned into **a labor of love.**

building traditional baths. He designed the bath and supervised the construction, but it was actually built by the local contractors and workmen who had restored the house. A heating device and thermostat were installed underneath the flooring so that when you leave the dressing area and step into the bathing surround you feel the warm stone underneath your bare feet. The ritual of the bath is ceremonially circumscribed as much for comfort and hygiene as for the sensual pleasure of the experience.

"Sitting in the steaming tub, it is refreshing to open the shoji screen and push back the glass doors to fully enjoy the outdoor scene," Kay says. "In the winter you can look out over a snowy meadow and see our twig gazebo, while in the summer, the field is full of flowers."

ABOVE LEFT: *Snowshoes propped on the railing ease the hike up to the Adirondack porch.* ABOVE: *A frozen pond behind the porch is ideal for skating parties.* LEFT: *A shoji screen, which slides back to reveal the out-of-doors, is reflected in the steaming waters of the bath.*

sea breezes

wooden classic

THE *DOUBLE EAGLE*, A 58-FOOT wooden boat owned by Michael and Jena King, has the sterling pedigree of a classic, launched as it was in 1948 from the legendary boatyard of M. M. Davis and Son of Solomons Island, Maryland—one of the first luxury yachts built in the yard after World War II. That it is now owned by the Kings has a special significance for Michael. "He was born in 1948 and so was his boat," says Jena. Now this "cold-water" Chesapeake Bay boat has a mooring on the southern California coast where the Kings ensure that it is still appreciatively used as a weekend escape for family and friends.

The Kings are a well-known family in the entertainment business. KingWorld was started by Michael's father when he syndicated *The Little Rascals* in New York early in broadcast history. Michael and his brother, Roger, continued the family tradition by syndicating the popular game shows *Jeopardy!*, *Wheel of Fortune*, and *Hollywood Squares*, as well as the hugely successful *Oprah;* they recently sold KingWorld.

During the war, the flagging M. M. Davis and Son boatyard was revitalized with a military contract to design and build T-boats for transporting army personnel. After the war, these skilled boatbuilders and craftsmen once again turned their attention to building luxury craft. Not coincidentally, the *Double Eagle* has a hull modeled after the wartime T-boats, fastened with galvanized iron spikes and constructed of sturdy oak frames with fir planking.

Honduran mahogany paneling and furniture, including a curvaceous bar and wine cabinet, and a brass-plated wood-burning stove, helped dif-

OPPOSITE: *The flag unfurls as the* Double Eagle *heads out for another glorious day at sea.* ABOVE: *Pottery, fabrics, and furniture are from Lynn von Kersting's shop, Indigo Seas. The designer waves from the entrance to the restored galley-salon.*

| 103

ABOVE: *In the salon, striped French silk covers the banquette, which is strewn with hand-blocked cotton toile pillows. A pair of nineteenth-century hand-colored shell engravings hang on the wall. The mirror, cocktail table, and light fixtures are original to the boat.*

ferentiate the yacht from typical T-boat design and put it in a class by itself. Today the original appointments—electric fans, telephones, Seth Thomas clocks that still strike the hour, light fixtures, the complete tool chest, maps and charts—all remain in immaculate condition. The *Double Eagle* insignia is found throughout the boat, etched on mirrors and bar glasses and molded into brass plates to adorn doors and storage areas.

"Michael and I had our first date on this boat. There was never any question of changing anything. We couldn't disturb her integrity, her historic charm," remembers Jena. What the Kings did do was to hand over the keys to designer Lynn von Kersting and commission her to freshen up the boat and restore some of its former elegance and glamour.

"My efforts," says Lynn, "helped revitalize the grace and style from the era in which she was launched. What I tried to give the *Double Eagle* was a subtle hint of the tropics—now that she's in warmer waters—

without disturbing the peace and serenity that has always been her allure."

Traveling at a leisurely 10 knots per hour, the *Double Eagle* takes to the sea like a queen. Her heavy diesel engine, "full chest," and large capacity for fuel and water assure her passengers of safety and comfort.

Says Jena, "Our favorite destination is a weekend trip to Catalina Island. Nothing is more tranquil than the reassuring sound and motion of the sea lapping at her sides. Nights on the water off the southern California coast are fair and warm. There is always the promise of summer in the air, and we love to get out on her decks to dream, plan, unwind, and go wherever our weekend mood takes us. Everyone is carefree, happy, and completely at ease when aboard."

A wooden classic, the *Double Eagle* embodies shipshape discipline tempered by elegance and romance. From portal to banquette, wheel to aft, nothing is amiss in her perfection.

TOP LEFT: *The mahogany bar and stools as well as the fitted kitchen are all original features. The bar glasses are engraved with the* Double Eagle *insignia.* CENTER: *Heading home after a weekend cruise.* TOP RIGHT: *The Captain's domain in the wheelhouse.* BOTTOM LEFT: *The Double Eagle's log chronicles an illustrious past and glamorous present.* BOTTOM RIGHT: *Rose-strewn wallpaper and bold ginghams mix in the guest quarters.*

family
boatyard

SOMETIMES YOU HAVE A DREAM

that's been with you since childhood. If you're a hockey fan, maybe
that dream is to hold the Stanley
Cup in your hands. Maybe your
dream has always been to own a
boat and live near enough to the water so that when you feel like going on
a voyage you just have to step out the back door and onto your boat.

Others dream for their children. They want them to grow up with an
intimate sense of nature, perhaps on a farm, or in a house by the woods, or
in a cottage near the sea. These parents believe that such experiences will
impart to their children an appreciation of history, of how people are connected to those who have come before them. They want their children to
identify with those who worked the land and dreamed the same dreams
for their own children.

Peter Donahue, a die-hard New York Rangers fan, had, in fact, held
the Stanley Cup in his hands. He is also an avid boatsman, and with his
wife, Marilyn, wanted a family life on the water. With this vision in mind
they took over the family business—the Tide Mill Yacht Basin, a former
mill in the town of Rye, New York, which had been a private boatyard for
the Long Island Sound community since the 1850s.

The building where Peter has his office and runs the yacht basin dates
back to the 1700s. It was built across three dams that were established to
harness the power of the Sound tide. Years ago the incoming tidal waters
would fill the muddy bottom of the mill pond and be confined there
until, on the reverse tide, the pent-up water would surge out over the dam
and turn two wheels on which revolved four huge millstones. Two of

OPPOSITE: *A member of
the third generation
of Donahues at the Tide
Mill Yacht Basin
makes good use of the
dock boy's window.*
ABOVE: *A rooftop cupola
was added to the
mid-nineteenth-century
house during a recent
renovation and has
become a private retreat
for eldest daughter
Christine.*

ABOVE: *Onboard the family's boat,* Constant Dilemma, *the Donahue children prepare for a late-afternoon launch. The burgee bearing the insignia of the old yacht basin depicts the red building of the original tide mill.*

these old original stones now line the driveway to the Donahue home.

The mill was vital to the early economy of Rye and New York City. It produced as much as 180 barrels of flour a week from wheat from the colonies. Coopers made barrels for the flour at the mill's own cooper shop, and one old barrel still stands sentry to the dam.

Four Donahue children share their parents' dreams in a house built in 1860 that sits adjacent to the old mill. Ten-year-old Mattie and 13-year-old Willie scamper about the yacht basin doing chores: scrubbing the dinghy, pumping out boats flooded by rainwater, or assisting in getting a boat out of the yard.

Fifteen-year-old Joe enjoys family excursions on the boat but is otherwise at the age when he wishes to explore on his own. He sails across the Sound with his friends, mastering the sails as his father did before him. Eighteen-year-old Christine sometimes sleeps out on an island, a sliver of land situated in the mill pond. She paddles out there in her canoe and

LEFT: *Growing up so close to the water has given the children plenty of opportunity for adventure. With Willie at the helm and Mattie behind, the boys inspect the harbor aboard their Jet Ski.* BELOW: *A picnic waiting to happen aboard the* Good Mate, *a classic Hinckley Picnic Boat.*

LEFT: *The* Good Mate *in its slip at the Tide Mill. Perfect for the Long Island Sound environment, its maneuverability and shallow draught make it easy to anchor close to shore, so picnics on local islands are easily arranged.*

pitches a tent. Closer to home a rooftop cupola, added during a renovation of the house, is her own private retreat. There she can spy on her brothers as they play Ping-Pong in the yard and jump recklessly on their trampoline.

The setting does pose challenges. As Marilyn relates, "I was a nervous wreck when the children were small. When we moved in, Christine was just starting kindergarten and Willie was less than a year old. Being surrounded by water, I had to watch them constantly." Still, she says, "we were always outside doing things. My house was a mess because I was always with the children." Some would think that having a messy house is not a bad trade-off for that kind of family time.

A happy balance between work

The children also had strict rules to follow or there were consequences. "Life jackets on deck was rule number one," says Marilyn.

The house was small when the Donahues moved in. "We turned the attic into bedrooms for the boys," Marilyn recounts. "We actually had to do two renovations to accommodate our growing family. Still, living on the water was a dream come true for us."

The Donahues have established an ideal balance between work and play in their life at the boatyard. And when the family wants to escape they need only board their boat, *Constant Dilemma,* to enjoy the pleasures of life on the water.

TOP: *Mattie and Willie on the steps of the old mill.* ABOVE LEFT: *The circa 1770s building now houses offices, a shop, and storage for the yacht basin.* ABOVE RIGHT: *Airborne children are a familiar site at the boatyard.*

and play is possible in life at the boatyard.

beach
haven

SARAH SMITH IS A DECORATOR
from New York who knows something about small island life. She
has been summering on an island
off the New England coast for 23 years. Consequently, when people on
the island need to remodel or redecorate their homes, they often turn to
Sarah to work her magic.

"Decorating should be fun or you've missed the boat," proclaims
Sarah. This is how she is able to summer on an island and still continue to
keep up the pace she has established with her decorating business on that
other island of Manhattan.

"My life on the island has changed since my kids were small. Then, it
was tennis every morning, going to the beach, playing with the kids in the
sand. . . . They were incredibly laid-back, wonderful times." She isn't
resentful about the work she now does on the island because she enjoys it
so much. "I'd much rather work here than in Manhattan. Here I'm on the
phone with my feet in the pool." Instead of worrying about what time the
D&D Building (New York's design center) is closing, "the ferry schedule
dominates your life."

Sarah was excited to take up the challenge of decorating a circa 1920s
house on the island for a Texas couple and their young children. The house
is unique in that there are more doors than windows—18 in all—wrapping
around the perimeter of the house, and each is a Dutch door.

The trick to decorating this space was to "treat the doors like windows,"
says Sarah. "I used sheer curtains everywhere. I didn't want to block the
light." And the way the air whips the sheers as the breezes make their way
through the house is, she says proudly, "seriously cool."

OPPOSITE: *The table
strategically placed in the
mullioned-bay picture
window allows diners to
look seaside in this airy
Dutch-barn-inspired
home.* ABOVE: *Besides
picnicking, the family
windsurfs and sails off the
beach, a short flight of
steps below the lawn.*

ABOVE: *In every room there is an easy transition between outdoors and in. In the living room, the brick floor extends out onto the patio. Garage-style doors across from the delft-tiled fireplace open the room to the outdoors.*

"We didn't change the house structurally," says Sarah. "We made it open and free, light and airy; we made it really fun." She painted the interiors a pure white, even whitewashing the dark beams in the ceiling of the Dutch-influenced house to help bring the light and air inside.

"The delft tiles were already in the family room. I played on that color scheme with more blues and added some crisp white to reflect the sky on a sunny summer's day," explains Sarah. A centerpiece of antique blue and green glass fishing floats catches the light and makes their reflected colors dance on the surface of the antique pedestal table. A painted trunk expresses the nautical themes elsewhere in the room as does the lampshade with its undulating wave border. Large gingham-checked blue-and-white sheers play in the breeze.

A softly worn floor of brick seamlessly joins the brick of the exterior courtyard and makes for an undisturbed flow between outside and in when the doors are open in their summer mode. "Bricks continue uninter-

rupted from the interiors to the outside terrace. It really is a house that integrates the outdoors," says Sarah.

The casual atmosphere of the house is perfectly geared for a family that likes to sail and windsurf and play on the beach. A deck overlooks their private beach and is equipped with a hot tub in which to soak and watch the sunsets after impromptu picnics.

The family moved in just before the summer season began. Consequently, most of the interior work was completed during the winter and spring. "Our day trips out here were so cold that we could see our breath while standing in the living room," Sarah says. So enthused were the couple and their decorator about touring the house-in-progress that on one visit they missed the last ferry of the day. "We got so cold—but what else could we do? We went to the neighbors and got cozy by their fire." That's part of an island, too. "It's really smaller than a small town," explains Sarah. "People are very caring and supportive on an island."

TOP LEFT: *Dutch doors in this light-filled bedroom allow easy access to the outdoor terrace.*
TOP RIGHT: *A hand-painted lampshade mimics the waves beyond.*
BOTTOM LEFT: *Antique fishing floats in glimmering sea hues catch the sun's rays.*
BOTTOM RIGHT: *A collection of hurricane lamps awaits the dusk on the outside veranda.*

stylish sandcastle

IGNORING THE BIBLICAL ADMONITION to avoid building houses on the sand, David Lawrence Gray, a Los Angeles architect, has built enough of them to be a self-described beach house maven. An award-winning architect with a loyal celebrity clientele, David has avoided tempting the gods of fate by building his beach homes on a bedrock of steel, encompassed by concrete and glass materials that are themselves made of sand.

David has created this particular sandcastle on an exclusive stretch of southern California beach for the Slavin family. The home is comprised of two vaulted-roof structures. The first—facing the road—is the garage-cum-guest quarters. Descending slabs of concrete steps, flanked by gently flowing streams of water, lead to the second vaulted structure, the family pavilion, with the gleaming Pacific beyond.

The architect describes the effect as "a stream flowing to the sea. It begins with a spring fountain in front of the house and the water runs down the hill as you descend into the courtyard. It is a moving sculpture representing the flow of fresh water merging with the sea."

Businessman Ted Slavin and his wife, Carole, are serious art collectors and are very involved with the Los Angeles art community. Their beach house reflects their interest in contemporary American pieces, while their home in Brentwood contains a fine collection of older and more traditional American, European, and folk art.

As collectors, Ted and Carole took the choice of architect for their beach house project seriously and found that David meshed with them

OPPOSITE: *An antique console table displays beach finds and other collectibles. The low furniture was designed deliberately to offer unobstructed views of the Pacific beach.*
ABOVE: *The front entrance expresses the building materials throughout—concrete, glass, and steel.*

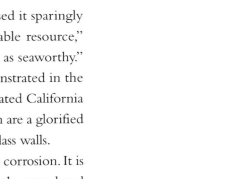

creatively. Carole explains that "low maintenance was one of our biggest priorities. I've been to beach houses where you can never seem to be rid of the paint crews. I was leery of the idea of a concrete house until David showed us one he'd built in Beverly Hills. It was stunning and he made me a convert. I'm thrilled we built in concrete."

David elaborates, "With the steel, which is covered with the same kind of paint used on deep-sea oil rigs, and the concrete and glass, we've found a vocabulary that will weather the brutal sea-salt sprays. As they age, the materials will acquire a patina that makes them look better. There will be a graceful and gradual maturing of the materials."

Some of the interior walls are finished in teak. "We used it sparingly on the ceiling and as paneling because it is a nonrenewable resource," David says. "It softens the other materials while being just as seaworthy."

The textures, tonalities, objects, and sensibilities demonstrated in the Slavins' living quarters contain all the elements of sophisticated California design. The living room, adjoining dining room, and kitchen are a glorified cabana, an oasis of shade for the forces at play beyond the glass walls.

A custom-designed dining table of glass and steel resists corrosion. It is paired with chairs by Michael Taylor, with the result that the wood and fabric of the chairs soften the table and surrounding concrete walls.

"I had the help of Sheri Schlesinger, an interior designer in Los Angeles who was brilliant at assisting me in making this house come together,"

The house is not that large, but there

is an **enormous** sense of space.

ABOVE: *A large outdoor living space helps create a smooth transition from house to dunes to beach. Bold built-in concrete banquettes are covered with canvas duck cushions. A hot tub is strategically placed to capture ocean views, yet be part of the conversational hub.*

says Carole. "We successfully incorporated our art collection while making it informal and easy for summer entertaining and young children."

Sheri explains, "We needed to warm up the house in contrast to the concrete. We ultimately found the right balance by mixing antiques—the large console table, the rugs—with larger contemporary pieces. We put together things the Slavins loved, and always followed the dictum that everything must be fully usable and absolutely comfortable. We didn't want anything that would get wrinkled or ruined from sand or salt water when someone sat down in it after coming in from the beach."

"Every weekend," continues Carole, "it's nonstop entertaining. The house is not that large, but there is an enormous sense of space. We incorporate the interior, the patio, and the beach areas when we have friends over. During the summer we have barbecues and people can lounge wherever they feel comfortable. It is truly our summer home—all year round—and we can hardly bear to leave it. Everybody loves it here."

TOP LEFT: *In the architect's vision, fresh water becomes a living, moving sculpture in this stream flowing adjacent to the path leading to the front door.* TOP RIGHT: *An African shell-embroidered pillow.* ABOVE: *A fossilized nautilus becomes a decorative element on a concrete side table on the patio.* LEFT: *A natural landscape of sea grasses in the dunes along the boardwalk from the beach to the house.*

paradise
found

TONI MORRISON WROTE AN acclaimed book about a group of kinsmen looking for a place to call home. When these righteous souls think they've found it, they name their town, with optimistic gratitude and pride, Paradise.

A Nobel Laureate, Pulitzer Prize—winning author, peripatetic lecturer and teacher, Toni Morrison travels widely and maintains several residences. At Princeton University, where she is the Robert F. Goheen Professor, she has a town house, and in New York City, the hub of the publishing and media worlds, she has established a pied-à-terre in a historic old building downtown. But for Toni, paradise is found in a rebuilt converted boathouse in a small hamlet on the Hudson River not far from New York City.

With the magnificent Hudson as backdrop, surrounded by her vast collection of books, photo memorabilia of family, friends, world leaders, and dignitaries, and an interior that exudes calm in its spare and quiet furnishings, it is here that she feels she has come home.

From an early-morning sunrise and a midday repast, to late-afternoon letter writing and contemplation at dusk, serenity emanates from the open porches, the cool flagstone terraces, and the dock that gently sways.

When asked about her getaway, Toni reflects that it's not so much about leaving and going someplace else; rather, "It's a vision of a place you've had in your mind all along. When you find yourself there, you recognize it. It's almost as if you've been away and in this place you meet yourself again."

The four-story "river house" has spectacular views of the Hudson from wraparound porches on every level. Here, the volatile seasons of the Northeast—the golden summer days, the blustery February ice storms—create a constantly changing and always fascinating tableau to be viewed

OPPOSITE: A nineteenth-century portable seaman's desk has found a literary home. It is put in place for letter writing here on the upper deck of Toni's house. ABOVE: The original inkwell and leather compartments meld easily with twentieth-century writing accoutrements.

from the decks and windows. In the summer months, sailboats and a potpourri of watercraft enliven the river scene. Fishermen set crab pots at the end of the dock and offer her the catch of the day. Every autumn, foliage bursting with color lights up the hills and palisades across the river.

In 1993, a few weeks after receiving the Nobel Prize, Toni was notified that her riverside home had been completely leveled by a devastating fire. Certain that this was the place that nourished her—the place where she had raised her sons and received the inspiration for many of her books—she was determined to rebuild. Her new house, though clean and modern in design, retains the essence of the original boathouse and was rebuilt in the same footprint as the former house.

If not better the second time around, the new house reflects Toni more personally—it was built for her and appointed with choice objects that speak to her soul. Besides arranging the exquisite interior spaces, she planned and landscaped her sloping lawn with multilevel flagstone terraces, boulders placed to look as though they were tossed up by the river, flower and herb beds, and magnificent containers of boxwood and lisianthus, geraniums and ivy, delphiniums and daisies.

On a lower deck just off the library is a hanging porch swing that, curiously, does not face the river view. Rather, it is positioned to capture a long, deep view of a shaded thicket, the foreground of which is landscaped and planted. "With the river constantly commanding your attention, your thoughts can wander off," explains Toni. "I wanted a vista that could contain my imagination, allow me to think inward. One morning when the boys were young I came out here, feeling drained and tired, needing to refocus my thoughts. I saw her come out of the water at the end of a path, and it was clear she was the character who would complete the book. She was Beloved."

ABOVE: *The new dock—here at daybreak—
was replaced in the footprint of the old and extends
into the river. It makes the perfect spot for river
gazing or daydreaming from an early-twentieth-
century steamer chair of bamboo and rattan.*

It's almost as if you've been away and in

BELOW: *This totem was an inspiration for a renowned passage in* Beloved. BELOW RIGHT: *Luncheon is served for a small group of friends on the sun-dappled flagstone terrace adjacent to the library. The water lapping just a few feet away offers soothing rhythms throughout the seasons.*

ABOVE: *Breakfast is served early on one of the three decks, each with stunning Hudson views. The magnificent river reflects with its own exuberance the drama of the changing seasons of the Northeast.*

this place you meet yourself again.

the high country

stone house retreat

IRA LEVY IS A PERIPATETIC entrepreneur, gifted at marketing and dedicated to good design. When he craves a weekend in the country, it is to no mere rustic retreat that he escapes. Rather, it is to an estate in the northwestern corner of Connecticut surrounded by rolling hills, sturdy farmhouses, stony pastures, and picture-perfect prep school campuses.

His house, "Deer Run," sits pristine and proud on the crest of a hill with panoramic views of fields and forests, the surrounding property dotted with 93 different species of conifers gathered from around the world, and small lakes intermittently visited by migrating waterfowl.

On this same piece of land is a separate guest house that was once a caretaker's cottage, a transplanted eighteenth-century "kitchen" cabin, and a stone, barn-board, and glass pool house with a slate-bottomed pool, which is nestled into the undulating landscape. These seemingly disparate buildings have in common Levy's notion of good design and meld effortlessly into his vision of eclecticism—all judged with his discerning eye. The simple pool house is the relaxed play-partner to the main house, a classic Palladian villa of which it is a part.

It is to the pool house that Ira turns for retreat and relaxation. "Going to this stone house can be an all-day outing. I'll pack a picnic hamper and walk down the hill to the pool. It's like going to camp. When I have guests, we swim, shower, dress, and then tuck into a luncheon brought from the main house, and we'll have big barbecues at night. At the end of the day we return home to our house up the hill."

OPPOSITE: *An aesthetic mix of American antique furniture, pottery, and paintings is characteristic of Ira's design tastes.* ABOVE: *A find from a Vienna auction house is mounted on a vertical beam.* OVERLEAF: *Local stone paves the floor of the pool house and extends poolside. The former stable opens up like a pavilion.*

It is to the pool house that Ira turns

for retreat and relaxation.

TOP LEFT: *A vertical slice in the end of the stone wall faces the east-west axis, making the pool house the perfect spot to appreciate the summer solstice and the winter equinox.*
TOP RIGHT: *A home-made plum tart marks the end of summer.*
BOTTOM LEFT: *Water trickles into the pool much like a Zen fountain.*
BOTTOM RIGHT: *An Indonesian backpack hangs from Shaker-style pegs.*

A horse stable with three stalls once stood where the pool house is now. "The stable was a fairly recent structure, built in the 1950s," explains Ira, "and it didn't particularly lend itself to renovation. But the configuration of the original stable was very well designed, nestled into the hillside without imposing itself on the views to or from the main house. When we tore the stable down I had the pool house built in the exact proportions as that old stable."

In New England it is a sensory treat to be able to swim out-of-doors six months of the year, coaxing the pool into retaining heat for that final swim in late October when the hills are ablaze with color and an afternoon dip concludes with a hot mug of coffee and a slice of an inviting plum tart. The mix of cool air and warm water, of breathing in hints of snow while your skin emits steam—this is what is meant by invigorating. "It feels rather Scandinavian and healthy," says Ira, "and I always come out feeling more relaxed."

Ira's design preferences are evident everywhere on the property, and

the pool house is no exception. As a former trustee of the Museum of American Folk Art and a vice chairman of the Contemporary Arts Council at the Museum of Modern Art in New York City, Ira wanted the pool house to have a spare and dappled coolness evocative of Shaker, early American, Japanese, and folk art influences. Shaker-style peg boards and hanging baskets blend comfortably and casually with an American-primitive trestle table. A windowsill is silhouetted with nineteenth-century medicine bottles, while carved coconut shells, found in a London junk shop, line another wall painted in what Ira calls "a lima-bean soup color." It has the look of great age and patina.

"The main house up the hill is more formal. Fortunately, the pool house does not share those manners or that formality. I love coming down here," says Ira. And, true to its stable origins, "Here I feel like a contented farm animal enjoying the amenities of my shady, protected barn and my pool corral. It really is like going to another place."

ABOVE: *A pair of Adirondack chairs positioned to enjoy the changing colors in the Connecticut hills. Ira often hikes the Appalachian trail, which borders the property behind the house.*

picture
perfect

THE VILLAGE OF LITCHFIELD,
Connecticut, is one of those
architecturally exquisite places
that filmmakers attempt to emu-
late when they create the perfect New England town for their films. Wide
streets with gracious and ample sidewalks are flanked by towering trees and
handsome, century-old homes. Artist Thomas McKnight, whose work is
known here and abroad, and his wife and partner, Renate, settled in Litchfield
in 1995 after dividing their time until then primarily between Palm Beach
and New York City. While still maintaining their city apartment, they now
find themselves gravitating more and more to Litchfield as their home base.

Tom's prints, paintings, and posters—instantly recognizable to his
many admirers—have been exhibited in more than 250 one-man shows
throughout the United States, Europe, and Japan, and his work is included
in countless private, public, corporate, and museum collections. Notable
among his many achievements is his creation of several official White
House Christmas cards.

Renate, originally from Austria, met Tom while vacationing in Greece
and they both agreed that first evening to spend the rest of their lives together.
That was in 1979. For the past 19 years, she has managed Tom's career.

The McKnights discovered their house—a stunning Colonial Revival—
while driving through Litchfield during a vacation in nearby Stockbridge.
"We both knew this was the house we wanted," recalls Tom. "I called the
local real estate agent and told him if it ever came on the market we would
be very interested. Shortly after it did, and we bought it."

After making the requisite structural changes, Renate and Tom set out
to create a home that satisfied their myriad requirements: a retreat from

*OPPOSITE: A built-in
niche in the attic studio is
used to store meticulously
arranged brushes and
paint tools. Religious
icons—this one from
Russia—appeal to Tom's
artistic sensibility. The
painting is one of his own.
ABOVE: A leather-bound
sketchbook on Tom's desk,
framing a dramatic view
of the Litchfield hills.
OVERLEAF: Tom's attic
studio, gleaming white,
is light-filled and airy.
A circular metal stair-
case leads to his private
rooftop retreat.*

installation of Tom's **light-filled studio.**

RIGHT: *The white porch and furniture make a cool, pleasant backdrop for the flowers and greens of the surrounding gardens and countryside. Here Tom, Renate, and faithful friend Shadow take a relaxing break at the end of the day.* OPPOSITE: *American vernacular—a pair of wicker chairs catch the late-afternoon light, which continues down the long path of greenery toward the hills beyond.*

their hectic work and travel schedule, a studio for Tom, an office for Renate, and a place to entertain friends. The house was originally built in 1910 for William S. Chase, owner of Waterbury Brass, Copper & Company. Wonderfully spacious rooms on the first floor are filled with the quiet elegance of Beidermeier pieces collected over the years by the McKnights, offering a perfect setting for Tom's paintings, which are hung throughout this superbly crafted house. All the floors have been stripped and polished to a honey-tone finish, save his studio.

Off the living room, a classic American veranda (the McKnights have seated 70 people for dinner there) looks down to a broad expanse of lawn bracketed by rows of large trees planted to create a visual allée to the end of the property. The Olmstead Company (of Frederick Olmstead fame) designed the original gardens and pond.

This porch also provides Renate and Tom with a quiet and secluded setting for reading on a chaise or having a relaxed breakfast. Sturdy wicker furniture and blue-and-white-striped cushions are arranged in comfortable seating areas; a pair of wicker chaises oversees the panoramic views of the rolling Connecticut hills. A freshly painted blue floor and ceiling complete this tableau of Americana.

The installation of Tom's studio in what was formerly the attic was the most dramatic change the McKnights made. The entire top floor was gutted and a widow's walk was constructed on the top of the house. Tom, who has devoted himself to painting full-time since 1972, explains, "I try to integrate what is real about a place with its underlying truth—its invisible soul—to create a catalyst for emotions, whether it's nostalgia, joy, or the sadness of time passing."

malibu oasis

STRETCHING OUT RELAXED, long, and lean on a Malibu hillside, the home of Buzz Yudell and Tina Beebe celebrates the agrarian heritage of the land on which it stands. It fancies itself a farmhouse, with the surrounding chaparral transformed into a series of cultivating beds and fruit groves. "This was once a tomato field," explains Buzz. "The house and gardens are set into an agricultural landscape, now planted with more diversity." And diverse it is, with a harvest that yields overflowing baskets of limes, oranges, olives, quince, pomegranates, figs, and grapes; and buckets of zinnia, delphinium, and numerous herbs—lavender, sage, rosemary, scented geranium, and nasturtium among them.

Suggesting influences from Mexico, Italy, France, the American Southwest, and New England, this is the haven that Buzz and Tina have created as their own. Residing much of the week nearer their joint offices in Los Angeles, the couple—he an architect, she a landscape designer and colorist—yearn for time spent at the "farmhouse" that he designed and built and she planted with the colors and forms of the landscape. Their shared dream, now realized, was to return the property to its farming origins while creating a retreat in the Santa Monica mountains with a view of the Pacific Ocean.

"I can't wait to get back here at the end of the day or at the end of the week," sighs Tina. "We've been known to take our vacations right here at home." Indeed, there is a quiet serenity and a sensual richness that flows through the house. With walls doubling as doors and interiors continuing the interplay of space, orientation, and landscape, the house has the feel of an oasis—cool and inviting, stimulating yet serene.

Bordered by a walled driveway and a dry creek bed, the stuccoed,

OPPOSITE: *The golden southern California sun gives the terrace the ambience of eternal summer. Generous curtains create the feeling of a private room.* ABOVE: *The living room's mix of antiques and modern furniture reflects Tina's preference for soft color.*

RIGHT: *A Mario Bellini sofa and chair against a living room wall. The color was mixed by Tina directly into the wet plaster as it was troweled on.* BELOW: *A conversational grouping around a mosaic-tiled table bordering the main "street." The flowers were arranged by Tina with cuttings from the many gardens.* OPPOSITE: *A beaded lampshade sits on a nineteenth-century tole tray table.*

adobe-colored house steps down into the middle of the 100-foot-wide by 600-foot-long site. Buzz explains, "It was built along a north-south axis to take advantage of the amazing mountain views toward the north and the ocean to the south."

Entering the property from the north parking area, one walks south through a series of external courtyards lining a path that runs along the western wall of the house. The pool in the distance plays the role of central fountain, while a tented pavilion offers the seduction of a café repast. The visual treat extends past the olive groves to the ocean beyond. "The smells here are phenomenal," confesses Tina. "The perfume in the pergolas is dizzying when the flowers are in full bloom."

The surface material, both indoors and out, is Vincenza limestone. Ample-sized French doors link the living room to the outdoor patio areas. The colors and moods of the outside areas are reflected in the interior: furniture pieces are upholstered in monochromatic whites and beiges, while colorful accents resonate from pillows, lampshades, carpets, and the fruits and flowers from the garden.

"We've tried to design the spaces here so that you feel the same comfort level inside and out," says Buzz. "This house is designed to maximize the gentle, favorable climate so that we can enjoy both the house and the landscape around it, so that they become inseparable from each other."

ABOVE: *With the pool at the base, the north-south line of the property is accentuated by the steps, or "street," that runs up the slope of the hill past the house, patios, and gardens.*

Indeed, there is a quiet serenity and a

BELOW: *The tented pavilion offers shade and comfort beside the lap pool. Baskets of citrus fruits and pomegranates suggest a market stall in an ancient city.*

TOP: *Huge pots of succulents and a terraced wall crowned with roses line the steps from the house.* ABOVE: *A basket of freshly picked limes from the citrus grove at the top of the site.*

sensual richness that flows through the house.

bucolic
site

JENNIFER AND JAMES D'AURIA'S weekday lives in Manhattan are crowded with meetings, deadlines, and dinner with friends. James heads his own architectural firm and Jennifer serves as his chief financial officer when she is not pursuing her acting career as a regular on the popular soap opera *The Guiding Light*.

For years the D'Aurias owned a small weekend house that they loved in the coastal town of East Hampton, about 100 miles east of New York City. But they shared a vision of their ideal weekend retreat.

"I wanted something off a country road in a meadow with rolling hills and rural views," says Jennifer. The house James had in mind was "something barnlike but with a modern edge." He wanted the house to relate to the shingle style common in the Hamptons but he definitely didn't want a traditional design. Jennifer's desire for country and fields relates back to her childhood in Heresfordshire, England, while James's design aesthetic was inspired by his Italian heritage and, in particular, his admiration for the Tuscan landscape and its architecture. Not far from East Hampton, in the sleepy town of Amagansett, the D'Aurias discovered the perfect setting for their new home.

Jennifer recollects, "I was driving on the back roads of Amagansett during a wild rainstorm. I slowly realized the country road was right, the hills were right, and then I spotted a For Sale sign. I went back to where we were staying, got James, who happened to be sick with a fever, and bundled him off to the site. We both knew this was it."

James, who studied at the University of Florence and at the Pratt

OPPOSITE: A view through the house is offered from the front steps, encompassing the foyer, dining table, second-floor studio, and the wheat fields beyond.
ABOVE: The long pine harvest table is set for an evening repast and crowned with fresh-cut summer lilies.

Institute of Architecture, designed the home on a double axis to create two corridors of light. The design plays up the open, airy spaces and the unobstructed views of the surrounding fields that had been left fallow for many years before the D'Aurias bought the property. Once the house was finished they hired an organic farmer to sow their fields with winter rye so that their view of the countryside would look lush and golden year-round.

The Italian influence is evident in the dark, hand-rubbed mahogany floors and the stone patios. Steel beams have been used throughout to suggest traditional exposed wood beams, but with the harder edge that James favors. Steel is repeated in many of the design details. "James loves the idea of leaving the construction details exposed," says Jennifer. And it is no accident that their kitchen takes up a substantial amount of floor space. "My husband is an absolutely fabulous cook," she says. Bordering the agricultural belt of Long Island, the D'Aurias have access to ample fresh produce and indigenous ingredients direct from the farm. Fruits, vegetables, cheeses, even wines are made or grown locally. Gathering and cooking the bounty is one of the greatest pleasures of their weekend.

The D'Aurias didn't compromise when it came to appointing their kitchen gathering spot with state-of-the-art cooking appliances, a long marble work/breakfast bar, and a 16-foot, rustic pine harvest table. "Through cooking James truly escapes the pressures of life in the city," asserts Jennifer. "After one of his tremendous meals we hang out on the back patio, light a fire when it is cooler, and then just sit there and watch the stars."

The D'Aurias feel that they are a part of the surrounding countryside, and the house seems to meld into the landscape. "Here," says Jennifer, "you can see gorgeous sunsets, and dazzling thunder and lightning storms. Nature comes at you and envelops you."

BELOW: *A kitchen designed for serious cooking. An apron-front farmhouse sink is big enough to fill huge pots for boiling pasta. Upper cabinets are hinged from the top. Dual dishwashers ensure fast clean-up.*

BELOW LEFT: *A professional Viking stove with ample space for all the culinary accoutrements.* BELOW RIGHT: *A bounty of sweet peppers destined for great soup, salads, and sauces.*

ABOVE LEFT: *A long view of the clean-lined kitchen with ebony finished stools pulled up to the marble counter. Relaxed wicker seating is used at the rustic pine table, while the fireplace shares the chimney with its outdoor counterpart.* ABOVE RIGHT: *Jennifer and James in the kitchen.*

fragrant escape

A GETAWAY DOES NOT ALWAYS necessitate a journey to a beach house or weekend home in the country. For many of us it can be a room in our home or a secluded shade-covered edge of our garden. For Donna Kaplan, the antique-filled, finely placed bathroom in her Bel Air home has all the elements and accoutrements required for sanctuary and retreat.

"In this room I feel as though I'm a guest in my own home," says Donna of her bath. "It's wonderful to soak in a steaming bathtub and fill my senses with the various fragrances—scents of spicy roses and sweet jasmine—that waft through the open windows."

Except for indoor plumbing, generous water pressure, reproduction porcelain fixtures, and a multiheaded shower, this bathroom could have been plucked from a nineteenth-century French baronial estate. The accents are intentionally not modern and the ambience is more of a time and a place when cleansing was an occasion, enjoyed leisurely. Here one bathes in a room lit by candle and firelight, in water flecked with rose petals, surrounded by nineteenth-century furniture and fabrics, porcelains and glass, all from Donna's favorite shopping haunt, Indigo Seas in Los Angeles.

The authenticity of the antiques was a deliberate attempt to imbue this newly constructed home with genuine patina and age. Exquisite nineteenth-century French cotton and silk fabrics in stripes, brocade, and toile drape much of the furniture. A chaise longue and vintage comforter rest in front of the fireplace. An old Moorish writing table houses a collection of antique jars. "I relish every moment in here," says Donna. "It is thoroughly romantic."

OPPOSITE: *A romantic and aromatic still life for the bath—bathing salts, scented candle, roses, and French fragrance.* ABOVE: *The luxurious appointments include original nineteenth-century fabric on a tufted French slipper chair and a writing table and chair from Morocco.*

A getaway does not necessitate a beach

ABOVE: *On the inlaid table, treasures include an English porcelain milk jug, French crystal perfume bottles, and a silver dressing table set beside a more recent treasure— Donna's mother's recipe for candied yams.*

house or weekend home in the country.

memories

morning rounds

FOR HORSE PEOPLE—OWNERS, trainers, jockeys, and fans—time stands still for six weeks each year. Late summer in Saratoga recalls a gentler time: seersucker suits and sun hats in the clubhouse box seats, broad expanses of green grass on the infield tracks, and evening parties hosted by the storied names of horse racing: Whitney, Phipps, and Farishs.

Trainer P. G. (Phil) Johnson is part of the fabric of the season at Saratoga. A member of the Hall of Fame at the National Museum of Racing at Saratoga Springs, he has won over 2,100 races and his horses have won over $36 million in his 55-year career. He has an amazing record of 15 percent win from starts. So it is natural that, along with most of the horse racing "establishment," he makes the journey to this little corner of upstate New York with his horses and staff each July.

In 1998, Phil was given by the New York Racing Association (NYRA) the seasonal use of a small green cottage adjacent both to his stables and to the famed Oklahoma training oval, in honor of his status as a senior and universally respected member of the horse training fraternity. The barns and office were originally occupied by Paul Mellon's "Rokeby" stable. Now, this small, one-room retreat serves as Phil's base during his long days at the track, which usually begin at four o'clock in the morning and end after the final race, late in the day. From his cottage, Phil can look over his training schedule while keeping a close eye on the training oval. He can watch his horses working out, although usually he's right next to them, observing and directing amid all the action.

"A trainer is really the coach and the horse is an athlete—in the truest

OPPOSITE: Favorite photos of family, friends, and horses above Phil's desk, which displays some tools of his trade—stopwatch, binoculars, racing forms, and the Condition Book. ABOVE: The trainer outside the cottage that was given to him at the Saratoga racetrack.

sense of the word," notes Phil. "No trainer or jockey is any good without the horse—the horse carries us all; if he's a good horse we all benefit."

Like a coach, the trainer decides on the horse's activities and workout for the day. The groom then prepares the horse for the exercise rider, and the rider takes the horse out to the training track for a workout. "Like any athlete, if they've been working hard or have just had a race, I may give them a walking day. Others we're warming up for a race, or to stay in condition," explains Phil.

Saratoga is a family affair for the Johnsons. His wife of 53 years, Mary Kay, is the financial wizard and bookkeeper behind the scenes. Kathy, his oldest daughter, whom Phil taught to ride when she was four, won the prestigious Amateur-Owner-Hunter division championship at the Southampton horse show in 1973, and spends August in Saratoga with her husband, Don, and daughter, Emma. Twelve-year-old Emma accompanies her grand-

father to the track most early mornings and is a regular around Phil's Amherst Stables. His other daughter, Karen, is a reporter for the *Daily Racing Form*.

While Phil doesn't glory in his private clubhouse as much as he does in his horses, it is a respite from all the track activity and a place to store his private gear and track mementos. After the horses are fed and resting is when you might find Phil at his desk or sitting comfortably in the old leather Morris chair from the nearby vintage shop, Daphne's Antiques. Above the desk, which is the only piece of furniture that is original to the cottage, are pictures of his children, friends, triumphs, awards, horses, and special moments. A horseshoe hook hangs near the doorway with Amherst Stables' signature racing colors, deep blue and pink.

Upon his induction into the Hall of Fame two summers ago, Phil observed, "I always felt if anything good was going to happen to me in racing, it should happen in Saratoga!"

TOP LEFT: *An old Morris chair and a worn leather wing chair offer a respite for those rare moments when Phil is not with his horses.* TOP RIGHT: *Grand-daughter Emma on Bingo.* ABOVE LEFT: *Blue and pink "blinkers," signature colors of the Amherst stables.* ABOVE RIGHT: *Phil studying the forms.* OVERLEAF: *Early morning at the Amherst Stables.*

No trainer or jockey is any good without

the horse——the horse carries us all.

magical gardens

FRANCIS MASON'S RESONANT voice is familiar to ballet aficionados as that of the dance critic of radio station WQXR in New York City. He is also the editor of *Ballet Review* and the author of numerous books on ballet, including *I Remember Balanchine, Balanchine's Complete Stories of the Great Ballets, 101 Stories of the Great Ballets* (a best-selling paperback written with George Balanchine that is the definitive guide for the ballet newcomer), and, most recently, *I Remember Martha Graham,* which his previous editor Jacqueline Onassis asked him to write. His expertise and authority on dance is widely acknowledged and undisputed.

Another of Francis's deeply felt passions is for the garden that he has nurtured, together with his late wife, Patricia, in their Westchester County home. His gardens have been admired by landscape enthusiasts for miles around and are a favorite destination of the Garden Conservancy and Garden Club of America tour groups.

His weekend house—with views of the sparkling Long Island Sound on one side and the lushness of a nature preserve on the other—is reached in less than an hour from his Manhattan home. Designed by Sidney Rodgers in 1946, the house is renowned for the 24-foot-high garden pavilion addition designed by noted architect James Rossant in 1991.

The house initially belonged to his in-laws, Arthur and Leslie Michaels, who designed all the original gardens 50 years ago. Francis and Patricia tended to the maintenance every weekend, with the help of master gardener Rigoberto Monterrosa. In 1981, when it became evident that the gardens could use a little updating, Francis and Pat employed the great landscape designer Pamela Berdan. Francis describes her as "an indepen-

OPPOSITE: *A simple lattice strip on the wall is a catchall for notes, old photos, and Balanchine memorabilia.* ABOVE: *A special relationship: Francis and grandson, Dexter, stand in the former garden shed, now a writer's cottage and personal retreat.*

dent woman of means who designed public and private gardens in Manhattan." Pamela's suggestions for the garden included adding reverse curves to its formerly straight lines. She and the Masons also redefined the formal rose gardens by adding paths and "rooms" to their layout. A vegetable garden and a "boomerang" garden were planted near a Cedrus Libani. Filled with oranges and yellows in contrast to all the purples and pinks, the boomerang garden contained some of Pat's favorite flowers.

Like an elaborate ballet, Francis's property is a stage on which various moods and scenes can be played out: a rock garden was designed to give rise to the land and drama to the landscape; two bosky walks—walks lined with bushes, shrubs, and trees—were created on both the north and south sides of the vast lawn; a back lawn was established as a croquet court, with a gently raised slope perfect for that game.

Francis does most of his writing in a small secluded shed—formerly used for tools—situated at the rear of his property. "The floor and walls were

good. I just had it lined with weatherboard" to finish it as a studio, he notes.

This is where he has written for 10 years, surrounded by mementos of a glorious career in the arts. Ballet books, dance reviews, and tattered ballet programs are everywhere. A well-worn Smith-Corona typewriter is his writing tool. Old family photographs and familiar maps line the walls. "I feel wonderfully secluded here," says Francis. "It's perfect for writing. This is my refuge where I can get away from the telephone. In two hours in the morning or in the afternoon, I can write what in town would take a full day."

A worn bookcase and a typewriter table are among the treasures gleaned from the curbsides of Manhattan. There's also an American pine hutch table from his mother's collection on which he wrote his first book, in the 1950s.

With its sea breezes, the studio is cool on hot summer mornings, and it's heated by a little electric heater during fall and winter. "I can nap here—in fact, it's a great place to snooze on the plastic chaise longue I

ABOVE: *The circa 1820s clerk's desk serves as a practical work table and a handsome base for Francis's wire and wood bookcase filled with old tomes and photographs.*

ABOVE: *Dexter is eager to lend a hand, especially when the job requires digging in the garden.* LEFT: *A bench and a small koi pond nestled under a gnarled shade tree.* RIGHT: *Francis and daughter-in-law Julie enjoy cocktails at dusk in the Adirondack-style gazebo.*

found on the streets of the city." A wooden trellis strip serves as an easy display area for ballet programs as well as sepia photographs of family and friends, past and present. This is where I think about the past and entertain the future," confesses Francis.

During the summer, the main house is filled with Francis's children and his grandson. Dexter, his six-year-old grandson, is his constant companion outside as Francis weeds and digs and tends to the dazzling array of plants and flowers that inhabit the gardens. The property is lush and a stroll in any direction offers myriad visual delights: a Japanese garden near the fish pond; a small pool lined with river rocks; a larger pond filled with goldfish and frogs; a hammock nestled among the trees.

At the end of the day, Dexter joins his grandfather at the candlelit gazebo for cookies and milk, with cocktails for Francis. The magic is enhanced on Wednesday and Saturday evenings in the summer by a dazzling, Norman Rockwell–like display of fireworks, visible from the nearby 1920s, art deco–style amusement park. The fireworks are the grand finale for a week-end retreat rich in visual pleasure and echoing with the music of dance.

lazy days

DOWN A COUNTRY LANE in a small seaside community on Long Island, the cottage of designer Sig Bergamin blends comfortably into a landscape of graceful wind-bent trees and bougainvillea. Proximately close but feeling far from the bustle of New York City, his getaway has the same nostalgic feel as a picture-perfect Fourth of July picnic. "Its simplicity and unpretentiousness bring back the home-sweet-home feelings and memories of childhood," relates Sig.

Lazy days, porches, croquet, and lemonade: the cottage's inspiration is postwar forties, the time of America's first widespread affluence, when summers meant leaving the heat of the city to seek refuge by the sea. For Sig, a world-renowned designer who studied at the Faculdade de Arquitetura de Santos, in São Paulo, Brazil, this small town has become his adopted second home. And in his cottage, white beaded-board paneling, vintage fabrics, quilts, and a mix of Heywood-Wakefield furniture—along with bamboo, French café, and overstuffed furniture—enhance the charm. Whimsical touches abound: a collection of colorful handblown glass vessels, stunning black-and-white framed photography, forties kitsch in figurines and tableware, and simple found objects such as starfish and seashells. The design approach Sig uses for his clients works well in his own getaway; eclecticism, ethnic diversity, wit, and versatility are evident in each room.

The wide lawn is big enough for a family reunion, with plenty of mature trees for everyone to have a seat in the shade. Flowers in cutting gardens bloom in profusion, guaranteeing fresh bouquets throughout the house. Guest-ready, the cottage has plenty of beds and a "serve yourself"

OPPOSITE: The perfect mix of kitsch and style is the Sig signature: an airy entry with zebra rug, vintage ticking, and chintz. ABOVE: The door opens to reveal a circular arbor entrance gate. OVERLEAF: A pastiche of photographs of friends and family adds life to the enclosed porch.

RIGHT: *A medley of bottles and blooms on the windowsill.* BELOW: *Divergent colors and patterns in fabrics mix with various genres in art.* OPPOSITE: *Economy of space packs a sleeping loft, sitting room, shower, and sauna into the former garage.*

kitchen. But the room that sets the tone for the rest of the house is the room one immediately enters on opening the front door—a little sun porch that has been transformed into a most welcoming foyer replete with all of the owner's signature touches. "It's an ethnic mosaic," says Sig, "a place to display my art collections, books, and memories of my trips around the world." A country pine desk serves as a display area for his framed photo mementos, as do the glass mullions of the adjacent window.

Guest rooms on the second floor are the perfect combination of north and south of the equator: classic American country quilts and European antiques blend stylishly with the pizzazz of Brazilian objects and textiles. "We broke through the attic and opened a few windows so that the second floor could receive natural light and have a higher ceiling. We painted the entire place, including the floors, white," says Sig. The white paint underscores the simplicity of the rooms. The high ceilings also allow for transom light, bookshelf display areas under the high windows, and the addition of ceiling fans throughout the second floor.

An additional refuge within the house is a simple but luxuriously appointed bath, with plush terry towels, French-milled soaps, and a solid-

OPPOSITE: *Attic space was removed to raise the ceiling and bring more natural light into the second floor. White painted floors and ceilings make the vibrant cotton fabrics stand out.* LEFT: *Bears with wide-open arms welcome visitors to this guest room.* BELOW: *An antique railroad lantern and a collection of shells are simple adornments.*

brass and porcelain handheld shower—a French antique from the turn of the century.

For the overflow of friends, a guest house has been fashioned from an underused garage. Still sporting its double garage doors, it discreetly disguises the surprises inside: a queen-size bed in a sleeping loft, a cozy sitting room, a shower and built-in sauna. Like the main house, the guest cottage contains a kaleidoscopic array of decorative accessories—Brazilian hand-painted wooden fish and fishing boats, a collection of framed and unframed oil paintings, colorful beads, children's toys, a hidden refrigerator, a TV/cable setup and CD player, and all the necessary accoutrements to make guests feel at home.

While the main house and guest cottage both sport a summertime feel, it's during the winter season that Sig enjoys his getaway most. "Winter for me is the best season to be here, especially during Christmastime," he explains. "I love the snow, and the fantasy of a white Christmas brings such a poetic atmosphere to the season."

BELOW: *Industrial lighting fixtures and a tramp art mirror are sharply defined against the white beaded board in the bath.* RIGHT: *A nineteenth-century porcelain and brass shower fixture in the vintage tub.* BOTTOM: *Cologne bottles on a Victorian bamboo cabinet.*

It brings back the home-sweet-home

BELOW: *Antique wicker and leather-handled suitcases offer stylish storage in the master bedroom.*
BOTTOM: *The green lattice and rose-covered entrance to the guest cottage. A picket fence surrounds a small cutting garden behind the former garage. A shady patch of lawn beckons in front.*

ABOVE: *This corner of a guest room reveals art pottery from Sig's extensive collection as well as a series of fish and shell engravings.*

feelings and memories of childhood.

literary meditations

THE STYLISHLY EXOTIC MOOD
in the gardens and pavilion of
the von Kersting–Irving home
in Los Angeles also permeates
the interior of their house. A Moorish–flavored entrance hall sets the stage
for the enticing possibilities to follow. Turn right and you're in an oval par-
lor enclave of soft sea shades and shells, loosely slipcovered furniture, and
antique pillows. Take a left and you find yourself immersed in a living room
of cinnabar-colored silks and wallcoverings, with oil and watercolor paintings, Chinese lacquer furniture, and blue-and-white export porcelains. Pass
an old painted screen of the Eiffel Tower and a few steps will lead you into
the cozy depths and layered luxe of the library.

Intimate, evocative, intellectual, this is a place of meditation and sensory pleasure. It is filled with first editions and rare volumes, vintage 78s
and LP recordings of Maria Callas and Josephine Baker, framed letters from
Dashiell Hammett, Noel Coward, John Barrymore, and Cecil Beaton, and
autographed portraits of artists and composers.

Lynn notes that Billy Haines, the Hollywood gadabout and all-around
style-maker, was originally responsible for these deliciously eclectic rooms,
with their vivid, exacting detail made perfect for reclusive intimacy. His
extravagant design talent, reinterpreted by von Kersting's skilled hands, has
culminated in a library with seemingly endless layers of richness, color, texture, and patina, not to mention books, records, and more books.

The fireplace is the focal point of the intimate room. A round table
before the fire serves as a spot for dipping into books or enjoying a late-
night supper, while two wing chairs and a worn leather sofa with a kilim
cover offer seating or reclining options. A duo of end tables fashioned from

OPPOSITE: *A framed
letter from Eleanora Duse
to Colette hangs below
an Oliver Meisel water-
color and a black-and-
white photo of Igor
Stravinsky conducting.*
ABOVE: *Painted panels
of the Eiffel Tower
stand sentry to a library
filled with sentiment
and enchantment.*

RIGHT: *Old gypsy fortune-telling cards nestle in a silver dish with early nineteenth- and twentieth-century playing dice.* BELOW: *A cinnabar vase filled with lavender and rosemary shares a shelf with a pair of Kashmiri candlesticks with nineteenth-century French paper shades.* OPPOSITE: *The library offers an intimate dining spot in front of the fireplace complete with an Indian print tablecloth and a French paisley upholstered chair.*

OVERLEAF, LEFT: *The last light of the day shines on Lynn's extensive record collection.* OVERLEAF, RIGHT: *A nineteenth-century marble bust sports an old Chinese smoking hat.*

painted Chinese leather trunks, a sofa table, and an assortment of chairs serve as a repository for Lynn's collection of books. Fabrics abound: French and Scottish paisley shawls used for curtains, antique kilim coverings, an Indian cotton tablecloth, nineteenth-century fabrics on pillows and trim.

"Great design is not about size. Even a one-room apartment can be vastly livable, filled with wonderful memories," Lynn says. "It's about creating a place to recall. It's about hearing voices from the past through books, music, and letters, and carrying that voice forward. You create beauty and enshrine memories so that you can share them with family and friends. That's what this library is all about," she explains.

For Lynn and her family, some of the memories contained in this room are about the gentleness and innocence of childhood. "I'm surrounded by books given to me by my father, grandparents, and aunts. There are also other family mementos," she continues, "my father's letters and record collection, manuscripts from my days at the Actor's Studio with Lee Strasberg, and my own child's favorite books and drawings. These are beautiful things that have survived the test of time and that the outside world can't encroach upon. They fill a need and as time goes on they are a comfort and offer a wonderful sense of security. They enrich us."

You create beauty and enshrine

BELOW LEFT: *Blue-and-white porcelain interspersed with old busts of French composers rest atop Scottish wool paisley.*
BELOW RIGHT: *A tole tray with nineteenth-century Portuguese majolica, Venetian glass, and French fruit cutlery.*

ABOVE LEFT: *An English tufted leather sofa covered in Turkish kilims and paisley pillows.*
ABOVE RIGHT: *An old lantern stands beside a worn French leather chair and a Moroccan pillow bearing a sultan's signature.*

memories so that you can share them.

pacific
harmony

LA CASA PACIFICA, "THE HOUSE of Peace," was the private home of President Richard Nixon and his wife, Pat. A frequent destination for the Nixon family, their friends, and the President's closest advisors, it was often referred to by the media simply as "San Clemente," or the "Western White House."

Tucked in the foothills of Orange County, the house's traditional red-tile and stucco architecture today blends harmoniously with the surrounding landscape. The property, which includes a pool house, guest quarters, tennis court, gardens, and now vacant Secret Service cabins, is on rich green acres, situated to embrace panoramic views of the Pacific Ocean.

The original architect was Carl Lindblom, a Scandinavian immigrant who was inspired by the umber-colored California hills to conceive a design similar to the country houses of Spain. Built in the 1920s for Hamilton Cotton, head of the California Democratic Party, it was historically significant from its inception. Franklin D. Roosevelt, a close friend of Cotton, was said to have visited La Casa Pacifica on at least one occasion, arriving by train on a still-active rail track that runs on a narrow gauge between the ocean and the lower edge of the property.

Gavin and Ninetta Herbert are the current owners of La Casa Pacifica and are principals of Roger's Gardens, a renowned California home and garden center in nearby Corona del Mar. The Herberts are fully appreciative of their home's architectural heredity. With the sympathetic vision of Newport News, California, architect Diane Johnson, they have changed the footprint of the home to such an expert degree that now, more than ever, it recaptures the feel of a Spanish hacienda.

OPPOSITE: *A circular staircase from a nineteenth-century Parisian town house makes a graceful ascent to the mezzanine library. A paneled curtain at the entrance is made of antique silk brocade sewn onto new velvet.* ABOVE: *A Portuguese santo adds a scholarly touch to the mezzanine.*

RIGHT: *In front of the over-sized fireplace, a tole tray displays roses from the many gardens surrounding the house.* BELOW: *An exquisite pearl-embroidered slipper is an elegant case for reading glasses.* OPPOSITE: *A Louis XVI–style daybed sofa in quilted burgundy fabric is an elegant background for a collection of antique fabric pillows. An ornate tea caddy rests on a side table.*

Enjoyed by the Herberts and their children and grand-children, and shared with countless friends, the loggias and rooms surrounding the tiled fountain in the central court-yard are resonant with an abundance of activity and the sounds of bells pealing the hour in the overhead bell tower.

Ninetta, who always had a unique vision for her home, worked closely with Diane, who also designed a new wing topped by the mission-style bell tower. It encompasses the Herberts' private quarters, consisting of a generous bath and dressing room, bedroom, study, and a gracious sitting room. "The idea for the sitting room," says Diane, "was to give the Herberts a private, personal space to read, relax, and enjoy the incredible view." It's so charming that they often entertain houseguests here for lunch or dinner, served with the French doors wide open to the warm Pacific breezes.

"We wanted an element of surprise in the sitting room," continues Diane, "so we added a library mezzanine, reminiscent of the one in Profes-sor Henry Higgins's home in *My Fair Lady*."

Adding to the serene ambience of La Casa Pacifica is Ninetta's stun-

OPPOSITE: *Beyond the sitting room, a nineteenth-century dressing table is placed next to a serenely watchful santo.* ABOVE: *Etched glass perfume bottles, vintage roses, and a silver mirror on the dressing table.* TOP RIGHT: *A mission-style bell tower added during the restoration not only peals the hours but plays evening matins.* RIGHT: *An arched brick entryway to one of the many gardens.*

ning collection of saint statues or santos and religious icons. Placid beauties, admonishing nobles, bountiful goddesses, impish cherubs, and reliquary remnants adorn tables, mantels, patios, and courtyard. The aura of antiquity is further enhanced by graceful furniture—architectural remnants such as the circular library stairs found in a nineteenth-century Parisian town house. Exquisite old textiles are now fashioned into wall hangings, portieres, and pillows.

Fruit from the groves at La Casa Pacifica make their way into each room, along with roses from the numerous gardens. With its inspiring ocean views, its fabled past, and the Herberts' attentive and loving restoration, La Casa Pacifica is a gracious sanctuary with panache and style to spare.

al fresco

hollywood hills

TUCKED AWAY IN THE HILLS
high above Sunset Boulevard is
the essence of an exotic rural
place. Hidden from view, the
home, pool, and outdoor pavil-
ion of Lynn von Kersting and Richard Irving lie behind 20-foot-high
walls of rose-covered brick, sheltering palm fronds, and lushly planted garden paths. Redolent with the fragrance of countless varieties of lavender,
rosemary, scented geraniums, roses, and citrus, mingled with that of wood
smoke and the faintly green smell of lavender-infused fabrics and antique
furniture, the home, gardens, and pavilion are a heady escape from the
electric atmosphere of their Los Angeles neighborhood.

The von Kersting–Irving home is legendary. Once the home of the
renowned film director George Cukor, it still retains the sense of glamour,
mystery, and romance that defined Hollywood in the early days of film.
Tallulah Bankhead, Greta Garbo, Katharine Hepburn, Spencer Tracy, Cary
Grant, the Barrymores—these are some of the icons who enlivened dinner
parties in the main house and lunched poolside in the adjoining pavilion.

This pavilion area is a constantly evolving scene. Each season it changes,
depending on what is blooming in the garden, what is ripe on the trees, or
how the angle of the sun bathes the hillside. And it is ever-changing in a
design sense as well. With the resources available in her own shop in
Los Angeles, Indigo Seas, the imaginative von Kersting is constantly re-
creating her outdoor terrace to match not only the seasonal mood but also
her own bohemian sensibility.

In the fall, when dusk comes early, the pavilion is dressed for a late-
afternoon lunch that extends into the cocktail hour. With a beguiling mix

OPPOSITE: *The poolside*
chaise tucked in among
the citrus and flowerpots
was original to the
George Cukor household
of the forties. Lynn
had it reconstructed and
draped it with Moorish-
inspired cotton prints
and pillows. ABOVE:
Moroccan votive candles
on a wire wall sconce.

of Moorish cottons, Moroccan chairs, French bar stools and beaded curtains, nineteenth-century Moroccan pottery, vintage paper candle-lanterns, and garden fruits and flowers, the pavilion is poised for all to enjoy a "take-home" repast. Thirties swing music comes softly from a CD player nearby. This is an al fresco getaway that extends far beyond the Hollywood Hills—it evokes a casbah with the glamour of a Hemingway novel, the cool jazz of a classic film score, the wit of a play by Noël Coward.

Lynn says, "It seems that we're missing some of the mystery, privacy, and discretion in our lives that existed for our parents and grandparents. Since those priorities are disappearing, it behooves us to create our own haven for family and friends—to exact those pleasures from life in every way possible." This is the philosophy that motivated her to create this stylish setting, one that she shares with Richard, their daughter, India, and her mother, Patou, who lives in a small cottage set back into the gardens.

"You need to enrich yourself," says Lynn, "and you do this by taking your cues from Mother Nature: plant a tree or a new variety of a rose; care for pet chicks and allow them free access to your gardens; revel in the dappled sunlight; absorb wonderful books, music, and memories; or put together an impromptu picnic, with plenty of comfortable spots for repose and relaxation."

ABOVE: *The outdoor poolside pavilion in all its enticing splendor.* RIGHT: *A pool once graced by the likes of Hepburn and Tracy, various Barrymores, and Tallulah Bankhead retains its Hollywood glamour in the loving and capable hands of Lynn von Kersting.*

BELOW: *A Chinese porcelain garden stool is laden with ripe blood oranges beside a teak and rattan chaise.* RIGHT: *Circa 1920s French paper lanterns, many still fitted with original beeswax candles.*

ABOVE: *An old French bar and a beaded curtain doorway pronouncing "Maison" are a fitting backdrop for the ingredients of an al fresco luncheon.*

This is an **al fresco getaway** that

BELOW: *A burst pomegranate rests on a stack of French café dishes.* BOTTOM: *Moroccan pottery hangs on the white-washed brick walls of the pavilion. Moorish and Turkish cotton print pillows embellish the built-in banquette.*

extends far beyond the Hollywood Hills.

suburban
panache

THIS IS ONE OF OUR GETAWAYS.

My husband, Kevin, and I were fortunate enough to find a 100-year-old house—about 15 years ago—not too far from New York City, with all the wonderful charm and groundedness of an old house and a sufficiently bucolic backyard to give us the feel of a country retreat.

Beginning with the first suggestions of warm weather in the spring and lasting well into the middle of October, our family's activities—culinary, athletic, and otherwise—gravitate to our back lawn and the rooms, porches, and terraces that overlook a glorious stretch of green grass, the weathered old trees, and my prized English garden. Depending on our two sons' activities and interests, it also can be occasionally transformed into a touch football field, volleyball court, or practice golf range.

Our dining room—with its large round mahogany table and high-back chairs covered in pale green silk—has two sets of French doors that open onto a small brick porch with steps leading down to our backyard and garden. From April until the waning days of November a sturdy forest green canvas awning—with side flaps that can be unfurled to protect us, and sometimes our furniture, from windy rainstorms—covers the porch, creating a wonderfully protected and private space for reading, relaxing, writing, editing, and dining al fresco.

Every couple of years I love to change the porch's look. Out here I can be a little more creative and daring. Most recently I furnished it in a colonial "Anglo-raj" style, with great old pieces I'd discovered at flea markets, and I pulled it together with lots of pillows, candles, flowers, and plants. I

OPPOSITE: *Winnie waits patiently for others to join her on the terrace. A canvas awning protects this outdoor room from all types of weather.* ABOVE: *Candles cast a golden glow on this arrangement of sea treasures in front of the large dining room mirror that leads to the garden.*

ABOVE: *A thick cushion and plenty of pillows make a comfortable reading spot for Nicky while he cuddles Winnie on the Indonesian teak bench on the terrace. A pine chest holds the necessary accoutrements for outdoor dining—napkins, placemats, and lap trays.*

searched and searched and finally found an outsized Philippine bench made of teak (a wood usually found on boats and great for outdoor furniture) with a high hand-carved back, and I had lots of kilim and off-white, washable cotton-duck pillows made for it. My friend Carolyn Schultz found an antique bamboo cart that has space for a bar, and wicker and rattan boxes to hold candles and other tchotchkes. A pine trunk that's been in our family practically forever fills in perfectly as a coffee table and is great for storing those plump pillows and extra tablecloths. A catalog supplied a faithful fountain that splashes water when we plug it in, and in the evening, with soft music playing on the stereo and the shimmering light of votives, we feel we could just as well be in Tuscany or Nantucket!

A second, and probably more teenager-friendly, access to the backyard and gardens is through our family room—filled with books, comfortable sofas, and two honey-toned leather chairs—which is reached by the stair-

LEFT: *An iron and glass trestle table created by artist Ron Lessard serves as a buffet when dining outdoors. An antique beverage carrier holds mineral water. Lattice adds interesting texture to the stuccoed walls of the house.* BELOW: *A collection of Victorian specimen jars.*

LEFT: *A bamboo and rattan serving cart was purchased at an outdoor antique sale for less than the price of the beverages sitting on top.* OVERLEAF: *Another patio allows for larger groups of diners. A pair of market umbrellas provides shade and definition to the outdoor room.*

Simple mullion glass doors lead

OUT to a slate-covered back terrace.

ABOVE: *The candles are lit at dusk as family and friends gather for dinner.* OPPOSITE: *A lightweight, portable rattan table and a pair of chairs occupy a nook in the garden set for a quieter gathering—champagne and strawberries for two.*

case in our kitchen. This is an informal room for relaxation, reading, and television. (I even slipcover the sofas and change the pillows to a soft floral chintz for the summer months.) It has simple mullion glass doors that lead out to a large slate-covered back terrace, which is flanked by a cascading garden filled with fairy and vintage roses, lilies, astilbes, and, early in the season, deep blue irises—a glorious gift from my friend Nan Rosenblatt.

The centerpiece on this backyard terrace is a sturdy wrought-iron and glass-top table that can seat eight people for dinner. I looked long and hard for this piece and its matching chairs years ago when we first moved here, and now this terrace has even become a great spot for a quiet solitary breakfast. Two large canvas market umbrellas (matching the green shade of the upper-terrace awning) provide cover from the sun during the day; at night, highlighted by the lights of the pillar and votive candles on the table, they create a cozy, protected mood. For the dinner hour, I also amass small votive candles in an old stone birdbath in the center of the back lawn; old strategically positioned floodlights enhance the natural grandeur of the towering trees at the rear of our garden.

storybook
tree house

This is the story of two very lucky little girls. Sarah and Fiona are sisters who live with their parents in Croton-on-Hudson, a small town along the Hudson River. Sarah is the oldest. She once had an idea that she wanted her daddy to build her a tree house in their backyard. He said he'd think about it. He thought and he thought. And then he thought some more. In the meantime, Sarah gave him some ideas. She showed him drawings of the tree house she wanted him to build for her.

While Sarah was waiting and her dad was thinking, little Fiona grew and learned to speak. Soon, she was helping Sarah persuade their daddy to build them a tree house.

And then one day the daddy had an idea. He would make a tree house like one in the girls' storybooks. The house would look like a bear's hideaway at the top of a tree.

The dad got to work. Gathering the wood was very difficult. He had to ask his neighbors if they wanted wood cleared out of their property. It was hard work clearing the wood but he got to keep what he took away. He saved and saved until he had enough wood and sticks to build a tree house for his girls.

One day, a few weeks before Sarah was out of school for the summer, her daddy started to work on the tree house. She came out to watch him. She told him to make it two stories. He didn't. She told him to connect it to the other trees in the yard. He didn't do that either. But he continued to build it his way, like in the storybooks, and soon it was finished.

Sarah and Fiona were so happy with the tree house that they wanted

OPPOSITE: *The octagonal tree house wraps around a tree with a split trunk. The support beams were the most difficult pieces of wood to scavenge.* ABOVE: *The tree house is set for either teddy bears or children to enjoy a late-morning snack of cookies and lemonade.*

TOP LEFT: *It's just as much fun to climb underneath as it is to play on top.* TOP RIGHT: *Daphne pours tea for friends.* BOTTOM LEFT: *The house is sturdy enough for at least four adults and countless children and dogs.* BOTTOM RIGHT: *A pretty plate and Grandma's pitcher are reserved for special occasions.*

to have a party. They invited their cousin Daphne to come visit them from France to play in their tree house. They invited their puppies and teddy bears and dolls to come and celebrate with them. They all got together in the tree house and drank lemonade and ate cookies. It was a lovely time! The girls celebrated having a house of their own. Now they could play house or school, or pretend to have sleepovers in their very own hideaway in the tree.

Dad's version "Relentless campaigning by my daughters—'Make us a tree house, Dad'—is how this came to be," explains Justin Casson about the tree house he made for his two young daughters. "I didn't really have any particular design in mind. I knew I wanted to incorporate this tree in our yard that had a split at the base. I wanted the house to encircle a tree, and an octagon seemed the best way to do that." He ended up building an octagonal platform, nine feet, six inches across, which has been known to hold all the kids in the neighborhood at the same time.

"I think the storybooks I've been reading for the last nine years have been the real inspiration," continues Justin. "Books like the *Berenstain Bears* inspired me. That was the look I was going for . . . a storybook look."

Justin selected white cedar for the roof and railings, since he liked the sense of peeling bark. The underlying construction method is called "cross-lap joint." In other words, the joints aren't stacked one on top of another. "I cut a groove in the wood in order for them to interlock," explains Justin. Besides giving the tree house a nice finished look, this allows for more head room for play underneath.

The finishing touch was the rope ladder. "I used cargo netting," Justin says. "They make it for unloading ships but they also have it available for kids' play gyms, and I put it up there on purpose, for safety's sake. I figured that if you could climb up the cargo net you were probably big enough to be up there." Justin doesn't bother to explain the inverse of that rule—that if the rope is too difficult to climb, you may just be too big to be up there.

ABOVE: *Sarah, in straw hat, provided the inspiration and constant reminders for the tree house. Fiona, in the middle, helped. Meanwhile, Daphne is busy feeding cookies to her stuffed animal. Southwestern textiles add a homey touch to the rustic tree house.*

secret arbor

BOB LEVENSON AND HIS WIFE, Kathe Tanous, have created a richly textured, multilayered garden in what was originally a spacious but nondescript backyard in East Hampton, Long Island. "We put in everything," he recalls, "the rose gardens, the pool, sheds, and pool house." Lush rosebushes abound, mingling with potted containers that line the patio and pool deck. Thick green hedges create a brilliant frame around their yard's canvas.

A shady secret arbor—affectionately referred to as the "ginkzebo"—was Bob's special and passionate project. "I designed it," he says, "because I had seen these Adirondack-type shelters and I thought, 'Why not make one of living twigs?'"

He began by purchasing four ginkgo trees from a nearby nursery. Patience and planning, along with the four ancient trees and a roof of clematis and roses, are the essential ingredients of the ginkzebo. "It looked almost like it does now from the very beginning," explains Bob. "It took a while for the roses to climb but all the elements were there that first spring—the hostas around the ginkgoes, the pebble floor, the flowering vines."

Perfect for afternoon relaxation, the arbor is the ultimate outdoor room. It's been the site of several outdoor weddings and even served as a huppah for their son's wedding.

"Kathe and I always make it a point to sit under the arbor when the wall of lilac and the roses are in full bloom," Bob says. "Then we pour a drink and go out there and take in the heavenly smell of lilac. Our other special time is when the roses are in full bloom."

OPPOSITE: *A table and chair from Loom Italia/ Country Gear offer a quiet reading spot in the dappled shade of the "ginkzebo."* ABOVE: *Roses create a lush valance in front of the doorway to the shed.* OVERLEAF: *The gazebo overlaid with clematis and roses and anchored with hostas.*

Perfect for afternoon relaxation,

the arbor is the ultimate outdoor room.

ABOVE: *Beneath the entwined foliage, the bold geometrics of a kilim rug over the gravel floor reflect the rich texture of the woven furniture. Another kilim piece, a bench, serves as a side table to hold reading material and an icy beverage.* RIGHT: *A bowl of luscious fruit, a relaxing chaise, and pillows make this a tempting spot to recline.*

index

Page numbers in *italics* refer to illustrations.